Kevin Basconi is one of the g——— ———— ———————ment and insight goes beyond natural vision into a vivid dimension of the Spirit. In this insight-filled book you can learn how he activates his spiritual gifting and how you can activate yours! A must-read for those who are serious about seeing more clearly in the supernatural realm.

JOSHUA MILLS
Best-selling Author, 31 Days to a Miracle Mindset, www.JoshuaMills.com

In Habakkuk 2:1-3 the prophet writes: "I will stand at my watch and station myself on the ramparts; I will look *to see* what he will say to me, and what answer I am to give to his complaint. Then the Lord replied: '*Write down the revelation* and make it plain on tablets so that a herald may run with it. For the revelation *awaits an appointed time*'" (NIV, emphasis added). In *Unlocking the Hidden Mysteries of the Seer Anointing and The Blessings of Psalm 24*, Kevin *saw*, as a seer, what the Lord wanted to say to him and then he *wrote down the revelation* and made it plain in this book *awaiting this appointed time* to be released into the church so that others might *see* what the Lord is saying through Psalm 24. If you want to be released into the seer anointing that you are entitled to, this book may be your key.

DR. FRANK BILLMAN
Director of Equipping Ministries, Aldersgate Renewal Ministries
Faculty Mentor, Doctor of Ministry in Supernatural Ministries, United Theological Seminary

Kevin Basconi had a visitation from heaven. He was instructed that we are moving into a new season and new supernatural realms that have never been available before. He was given keys to activate and unlock this new mystery of the Kingdom.

SID ROTH
Host, It's Supernatural!

Kevin Basconi's new book, *Unlocking the Hidden Mysteries of the Seer Anointing and The Blessings of Psalm 24,* builds systematically upon what he has previously written in his first book on the seer anointing. After reading the manuscript, one word of the title was especially significant to me: "*Unlocking.*" That is really what this book is about, being released from what impedes the God-given ability to "see" and then engaging with the tools to walk in that ability.

Kevin is a seer. He has learned to unlock and walk in a dimension that most do not. But he is also passionate about helping others to be freed to see into and from the Kingdom of God as well. Seeing what God is doing is Biblical, it is real. By "seeing" how our Bible heroes functioned and why they could do all that they did. This book will unlock the "seer" *in you* so you can walk in what God has destined *for you*. There are powerful prayers of release; as you agree with them, that will literally happen! You will experience a release, an unlocking of the seer anointing in your life! A great read and even better application.

PASTOR ALAN KOCH,
Senior Pastor, Christ Triumphant Church

This book is a must read for those pursuing the seer anointing. It is a deeply personal and provocative account of one man's journey into the hidden mysteries of the Kingdom of God which are being revealed to the Lord's seers in this generation. Kevin reveals two powerful keys to those who would desire to receive an activation of or increase in the seer anointing.

As you journey with Kevin through these inspiring accounts of the Lord providing wisdom and revelation, you cannot miss his profound sensitivity to the leading of the Lord and the Holy Spirit. This spiritual sensitivity is absolutely essential for anyone desiring to fully receive the impartation given in this book. The second powerful key is obedience. Every act of obedience resulted in the Lord releasing an elevation in anointing and understanding for Kevin. Following these principles will position you to receive the impartation being released.

I encourage you to pray over and over the many prayers of activation. Declare each of the decrees over and over. These practices opened doors or revelation for Kevin, and they will do the same for you.

PASTOR JAMES DURHAM
Higher Calling Ministries International

Kevin Basconi is a very good friend of mine and has been for a few years now. And if there is anything that I know about Him is that He loves Jesus with all of His heart. He is a man who desires to walk close with God and is someone who has seen Jesus face to face. A friend of God. The revelation that Kevin releases in this book has been given to him by Jesus, Himself. There are keys that Kevin shares that will unlock and open your ability to see into the realms of the Kingdom. This book will catapult you into your own encounters so that you may continue to build upon your history with the Lord but not just through knowledge but by experiencing the presence of the Lord. I hope the revelation in this book will bring you into a closer walk with the Lord and that it may help you fulfill your calling and destiny that the Lord has for your life.

ROBERT WARD, ITINERANT MINISTER
Graduate of Bethel School of Supernatural Ministry in Redding, CA

While there are a lot of books written about the Kingdom of God, few carry the necessary spiritual weight to unlock the hidden mysteries of heaven. Kevin's new book, *Unlocking the Hidden Mysteries of the Seer Anointing and The Blessings of Psalm 24,* will undoubtedly encourage and equip you to rise up into the next level of spiritual maturity.

MICHAEL DANFORTH
Founder, Mountain Top Int'l and SOHL (school of higher learning)

It is a great honor and blessing to be a friend and fellow worker with Kevin and Kathy Basconi as we travel the King's highway sharing the love of Jesus Christ with those who are seeking to receive the revelation of God's truth. Kevin and Kathy are people of integrity who live the principles they teach. In *The Seer Anointing and the Blessings of Psalm 24*, Kevin shares experiences in his life and insights he has been shown into Psalm 24 and the seer anointing. Enjoy!

DR. STEPHEN R. RICHARDSON
Ordained Foursquare minister and medical doctor, retired

I have known Kevin and Kathy Basconi for many years. I am their pastor and friend and I know that Kevin lives what he writes about in his books. When I read his quote, "Jesus spoke to me as a man speaks to His friend", I knew it was truth! As you read the pages of this exciting book your heart will be captivated and stirred for the deeper things of God! You won't be able to put it down!

CAROL KOCH
Christ Triumphant, Children on the Frontline

Unlocking the Hidden Mysteries of the Seer Anointing II

The Blessings of Psalm 24

Unlocking the Hidden Mysteries of the Seer Anointing II

The Blessings of Psalm 24

KEVIN BASCONI

Unlocking the Hidden Mysteries of the Seer Anointing II
Copyright 2014 by Kevin Basconi
All rights reserved.

ISBN: 978-0-9960217-1-5

King of Glory Ministries International Publications 2014
King of Glory Ministries International
PO Box 903, Moravian Falls, NC 28654
336-818-1210 or 828-320-3502
www.kingofgloryministries.org

All Rights Reserved. No part of this book may be reproduced or transmitted in any form or by any means—electronic or mechanical, including photocopying, recording, or by any information storage and retrieval system—without written permission from the authors except as provided by the copyright laws of the United States of America. Unauthorized reproduction is a violation of federal as well as spiritual laws.

Unless otherwise noted, all scripture quotations are from the New King James Version of the Bible. Copyright © 1979, 1980, 1982 by Thomas Nelson, Inc., publishers. Used by permission.

Scripture quotations marked NIV are from the Holy Bible, New International Version. Copyright © 1973, 1978, 1984, 2010, 2011, International Bible Society. Used by permission.

English definitions are from Merriam-Webster's Dictionary
Greek definitions are derived from Strong's Greek Concordance.
Hebrew definitions are derived from Strong's Hebrew Concordance.

Copyright 2014 by Kevin Basconi
All rights reserved.

Cover design and layout by Kevin Basconi & projectluz.com
Printed in the United States of America

This book Is dedicated to

God the Father, God the Son, and God the Holy Spirit

without You Guys none of this would have been possible!

Table of Contents

Acknowledgements xiii

Introduction xv

PROLOGUE
Eyes to See and Ears to Hear xvii

CHAPTER 1
Heavenly Invasions 1

CHAPTER 2
God-Ordained Hidden Wisdom and Mysteries for Your Glory 9

CHAPTER 3
The Manifold Wisdom of Heaven 15

CHAPTER 4
The Testimonies of Jesus 21

CHAPTER 5
Blessed Indeed! 27

CHAPTER 6
The Metamorphosis of a Life 37

CHAPTER 7
A New Found Land 43

CHAPTER 8
Greater Glory 49

CHAPTER 9
Who Is the Messiah? 55

CHAPTER 10
Fiery Seraphim 59

CHAPTER 11
Daisy's Cabin up in the Wilderness 69

CHAPTER 12
What Is Normal Christianity? 77

CHAPTER 13
Unearthing the Hidden Mysteries of Psalm 24 89

CHAPTER 14
Discovering the Keys of Psalm 24 99

CHAPTER 15
Blessing I Will Bless You 107

CHAPTER 16
Ascending to the Hill of the Lord 115

CHAPTER 17
The Double Doors of Breakthrough 123

CHAPTER 18
Enter the Presence Behind the Veil 133

CHAPTER 19
Unlocking the Double Doors of Breakthrough 143

CHAPTER 20
Unlocking the Secret Gates of the Treasury 149

CHAPTER 21
Shaking the Gates of Heaven 163

Epilogue 177

Table of Prayers 181

Prayers of Activation, Impartation, and Declarations of Glory 199

Prayer of Salvation 209

Recommended Reading 211

About the Author 213

Contact the Author 217

Acknowledgements

I want to thank my precious wife, Kathy Basconi, for her enduring love, kindness, patience, long hours of proof reading, and unfailing help and support with the entire process of writing this book.

Because of you I am happy, truly blessed, and highly favored. I love you!

Introduction

Our hearts were full of great joy as we attended the high school graduation of our oldest grandson. The small graduating class of his Christian school sat on the platform of a conservative evangelical church. We had such gratitude for the Christ-centered education that he had received. How proud we were of our grandson! We watched and listened as speeches were made and pictures were presented that reminded us of the transition of the graduates from infancy to graduating seniors. The time had now come for the pastoral challenge to the graduates.

The pastor had been a part of the school in the past and now served as a member of a church staff that ministered to over 8,000 people. The talk was a wonderful invitation to the students of the importance of a Christ-centered daily walk with the Lord. Then abruptly he made an aside comment that startled me. He spoke of hearing a person at a worship service at another church crying out for "more of the Lord." As he reflected on that comment he said that this was certainly not something that we had to do. His evangelical tradition would not confirm that this was necessary in a Christian life. I find this very unfortunate. Actually the joy and wonder of the Christian life is that there is always more and the Lord loves to hear us "seeking" so that we will "find" more of Him.

Even during my days as a Baptist pastor I would pray the prayer of the Apostle Paul found in Ephesians 1:17. I like the New International Version translation of this passage. "I keep asking that the God of our Lord Jesus Christ, the glorious Father, may give you the Spirit of wisdom and revelation, so that you may know him better." Yes, there is always more to know about our Lord and His Kingdom and yes, you can ask Him for more.

You are holding in your hands the book by Kevin Basconi *Unlocking the Hidden Mysteries of the Seer Anointing and The Blessings of Psalm 24*. I encourage you to *not* read this book if you do not have a hunger for more of the Lord. If you are content with your Christian life then this book is *not* for you! Do *not* read this book if you do not believe there is more. Do *not* read this book if you believe we cannot do what the Bible reports. Do *not* read this book if you believe the gifts ceased after Jesus apostles died. Do *not* read this book if you do not want keys that will bring you closer to the Lord. Do *not* read this book if you believe that the Bible consists of simple stories of what others did and that we cannot do what they did.

If you choose to read this book, then be prepared to discover keys that will unlock more of the mysteries of the Kingdom of God and testimonies that will drive you to earnestly seek the Lord for more of Him. A great adventure awaits you in the following pages.

Paul L. Cox
Aslan's Place, Apple Valley, CA

PROLOGUE

Eyes to See and Ears to Hear

I loved what my friend Michael Dansforth (Mountain Top International Ministries) recently prophesied during a time of spontaneous worship. Michael is a proven seer prophet. He began to sing prophetically about how we are going to see things in a new way and how we are going to hear things in a new way. Would you want to see things in a new way and hear things in a new way?

Jesus spoke about this dynamic too. Personally, I want to see things in a new way and hear things in a new way. How about you? Actually this ability or anointing to see and hear in a more supernatural way is the earmark of our healing. It is the sign that we are growing into mature sons and daughters of the Most High God. We learn to hear the Lord well. We grow and mature and begin to develop our spiritual senses to see what the Father is doing in our sphere of influence.

I believe we have stepped into a new season and that our God is opening up realms in His Kingdom. Many of these supernatural realms have not been available to us before. I am speaking about the realms of glory, the heavenly realms—the very domain of God Almighty, Elohim. I am speaking about the realms of the seer anointing and the ability to have Godly discernment in all things. Do you believe that? Is such a dynamic possible at this hour?

I believe that it is absolutely necessary for us to see and hear well at this hour. We must discover how to see and to hear in a new way today. I believe God has some things that He has hidden and held back in the Kingdom of Heaven for such a time as this. These hidden mysteries will empower us to walk in the fullness of Christ and enable us to usher in the Kingdom of God the way the Lord wants us to usher it in and demonstrate the Kingdom at this hour. It is absolutely imperative that we learn to hear and learn to see God in a great and mighty way. We are going to need to see and hear things that we haven't seen and heard before. We must expect to go boldly where few men have gone before.

Yes, I said *learn* to hear. We can hear in more than one way. We can develop our spiritual senses to see in more than one way! Remember what the Lord said in Luke 8:10: *"To you it has been given to know the mysteries of the Kingdom of God, but to the rest it is given in parables, that 'Seeing they may not see, And hearing they may not understand.'"* Later in verse 18 Jesus encourages us to *"therefore take heed how you hear."* Clearly Jesus was teaching us that there are many ways that you can hear and perceive.

In the pages that follow I shall share hidden revelations from Psalm 24 and other scriptures that can help you unlock the hidden mysteries of the seer anointing in your life. You can learn to discern. You can learn to see and hear in a new heavenly way!

CHAPTER 1

Heavenly Invasions

The Lord has been doing amazing supernatural things in these last days. One night at a recent conference that we hosted in Kansas City, the whole meeting at Christ Triumphant Church literally went up to Mount Zion, the Hill of the Lord. Or, I suppose that you could rightly say that Heaven literally came down and invaded the realms of Earth! It was an amazing heavenly encounter. God is doing this more and more in our meetings. It is not so much that we go up or ascend into the heavenly realms but that Heaven comes down and invades our space. Many times these heavenly invasions occur during worship; however, I have begun to expect the Kingdom of Heaven to invade our gatherings at any instant.

The glory of God manifests in the meetings in a tangible way. Amazing miracles are happening through many ministers and ministries all over the earth. Really, what it's all about is that we see and hear and learn to discern what's happening in the heavenly realms and then God releases those same manifestations of His Kingdom here upon the earth. So, in my opinion, it's a new thing that God is doing in the seer realm. It is a new manifestation of the glory realms being supernaturally released by the Lord to and through His friends at this hour.

The Spirit of God is beginning to train and equip His people to see and hear in a new and supernatural way in these last days. The Lord is beginning to raise up mature sons and daughters of God who will be like Christ (Romans 8:19). They will learn to see and hear in a new way. They will see and hear what their heavenly Father is doing; and then, like Jesus, they will simply do those things and amazing manifestations of the Kingdom of Heaven will transpire. Miracles, signs, and wonders from the Lord of Hosts will begin to become much more common and plentiful. Are you ready? Are you willing? I know and decree this fact: you are certainly able through the power of the Spirit of the living God!

In the Twinkle of an Eye

When we come into that place, that supernatural place of God's presence and His glory, we begin to get revelation and to have supernatural understanding of these dynamics in the Kingdom of God. These revelations can totally transform who we are in Christ. This supernatural knowledge can transform our lives in an instant and in the twinkle of an eye. We can receive revelation; we can receive miracles; we can receive healings; we can receive all sorts of supernatural benefits in the seer realms. We can position ourselves to receive the blessings of Almighty God in the glory realms. God is still opening up to His friends His good treasure, the heavens, and He is raining out supernatural blessings today (Deuteronomy 28:12)!

As I've been praying about this supernatural dynamic, the Lord has spoken to me very clearly. He is going to do unusual miracles at this hour. Would you like to see God release unusual miracles in your life and into your sphere of influence? I'm believing for an impartation and an activation for you for unusual miracles as you read this book. I will teach the Word of God, and God's anointed Word will minister to you through this book. We have included a series of prayers of impartation for you to utilize as well. I believe these prayers are breathed into existence by the Spirit of the living God for such a time as this. They were created for you as you read this book. I believe that they are alive. I believe these prayers are endued with the power and impartation of the Holy Spirit which can be released to you as you pray the prayers aloud.

I'm going to take time to build a foundation; but I am believing that you will receive something new from the Kingdom of God. I am believing that there will be an impartation for you to step into the next level of the Kingdom of God. You can move from glory to glory (2 Corinthians 3:18). God can take you from glory to glory as your read the pages of this book. I believe that there is a grace for God to take the seer gifting that's already within you and to activate it to a greater level. You are a seer. Do you want to step into the deeper things of the Spirit? You can learn to see and hear in a new and supernatural way. I want to encourage you to just believe to receive. I know that God is going to do something amazing in your life and through you as you grow and learn to mature your spiritual senses as you seek to become a mature son or daughter of the Most High God (Psalm 57:2).

By the grace of God, the Lord has given me a little revelation and I've had some amazing supernatural things happen in my life. If you've read some of my other books—*The Reality of Angelic Ministry Trilogy*, *The Sword of the Lord and the Rest of the Lord*, *Unlocking the Hidden Mysteries of the Seer Anointing*, and others—you know that the Lord has been speaking to me about the seer anointing for more than a dozen years. The Lord began to instruct me to teach His people about the seer anointing going back all the way to 2002. It has been an ongoing process of revelation, understanding, and supernatural impartation. It seems that the more that I give away, the more that I receive (Galatians 6:7). Even God sows and reaps today.

A Seed Planted in the Ground

I am certain that the Spirit of God is giving a remnant of His people wisdom and revelation; line upon line and precept upon precept (Isaiah 28:10, 16)! I hope to share some of that revelation with you in the coming pages. I would certainly encourage you to read the books that I have just mentioned because the testimony of Jesus is the spirit of prophesy (Revelation 19:10). I'm mentioning these things briefly here since you may not be familiar with the ministry or my other books. However, before I start sharing these supernatural tales and testimonies, I want to share another very important fact.

On Valentine's Day 2014 the Body of Christ released a general into his heavenly home. On that day a lovely gentleman named Bob Jones put off his earth suit and went home to be with Jesus. It just so happened that they planted his earth suit right at the end of my street in Moravian Falls. Bob was buried there in the neighborhood in which we currently abide. Man, talk about the heavens opening up that day! Praise God! They were open before, but now there is a great increase in the perceptible open heavens in the area.

Bob is up there in Heaven! Dying is not necessarily a bad thing; Bob is doing great—he's got a new body, he's looking good, he's hanging around with Jesus these days (2 Corinthians 5:8). Bob's got this big angel of wisdom and revelation that's been accompanying him as he is sauntering about in the heavenly realms. He's getting the answers to many of those mysteries he didn't quite fully understand while he was a sojourner here on this side of eternity. Remember that the Lord is not the God of the dead but the God of the living (Matthew 12:27). I am not writing about necromancy; I am writing about true Kingdom life! We all have an extended family in heaven who loves us (Ephesians 3:15).

Here is what I believe. In my opinion, when Bob Jones was placed as seed in the ground, there was a release of something supernatural in the seer realms. The Lord opened something supernatural in the glory realms. I believe that there is a grace that is being poured out like a drink offering on whosoever will (Philippians 2:17). This dear man, Bob Jones, carried something that few people in the Body of Christ have ever walked in. But I believe that everybody can walk in a very high level of the prophetic anointing that I call the seer anointing.

Again, I want to encourage you to just believe to receive something from the Lord. It is a God-ordained time. It is a God-ordained hour, and the Lord is releasing to His friends good gifts from the heavenly dimensions (Matthew 7:11). We can learn to see in a new way; we can learn to hear in a new way! It is gift from God to His friends at this hour. Question: are you a friend of God, or are you a person who just attends church three or four times a month?

Millions of Mantles

I have written previously in the book *The Sword of the Lord and the Rest of the Lord* how I have witnessed the Lord's angelic host poised to place new mantles upon God's children. There are literally millions of mantles (what some refer to as anointings) that Elohim has preordained to be released to people at this precise moment in time. The heavenly mantle of the seer is available to you. You can begin to learn to see and perceive heavenly truths and to enter into the Holy of Holies. You can go behind the veil and witness the realm of God's glory and the heavenly places today. I believe that this book may be a tool that the Lord of Hosts uses to activate this Kingdom dynamic in your life! Are you willing?

And for whatever reason, I feel the Lord has called my wife, Kathy, and me to declare this message. (It occurs to me that He has also given us the grace to have it heard as well)! Since the Lord appeared to me on November 25, 2001, face-to-face, He commissioned me to trumpet this message! The Lord instructed me to teach about the seer anointing and to pray for impartation for His people. We are to instruct the saints and to teach and train those who *can receive* from us. Right now I want to stop for just a moment and say this: although it is biblical, you don't necessarily have to have someone lay hands on you to receive impartation or activation of your spiritual gifting. I do not need to physically lay my hands upon you for impartation; nor does anyone else. You can receive impartation and activation as you read this book.

You may not need to travel to a "revival" in another state or nation. You can receive impartation from the Spirit of God, right where you are reading this at this instant! You can receive impartation anywhere on earth as you pray the prayers of impartation that are contained in this book.

Prayer for Eyes to See and Ears to Hear

Father, thank You for sending Jesus, the King of Glory. Thank You, Father, that through the shed blood of Jesus Christ and through the finished work of the Cross of Calvary, You have made us kings and priests who can come boldly before the throne of grace. Thank You, Father God, that the blood of Jesus make us righteous and Holy to minister to our God and Father. Lord, as I share Your word, I ask You that it would go forward in power and that it would not return void—that it would pierce the hearts of those who read it. Lord, I ask that as I share the Gospel and the testimonies that You have placed upon my heart, that there would be an activation and impartation of the seer realm which would come upon people's lives and that they would have ears to hear and eyes to see— that our eyes would see and our ears would hear things that we would not have imagined possible. Father, I thank You that we have stepped into a new dispensation of time, that You are doing amazing things in the earthly realms. Father, I thank You that the Kingdom of Heaven is truly invading our sphere of influence. And we promise to give You the praise and all of the honor and the glory for everything that You've done and everything that You are going to do; in Jesus mighty name, Amen. Hallelujah!

Now that I have encouraged you and sought to raise your expectation let's begin to get to the crux of the issue! Let's begin to look at several supernatural testimonies that will serve to increase your faith to begin to see and hear from the heavenly realms and to activate the blessings of the seer anointing and the hidden blessings of Psalm 24 in your life! Amen.

CHAPTER 2

God-Ordained Hidden Wisdom and Mysteries for Your Glory

In the coming pages I want to share some supernatural revelation with you about the hidden anointing and the hidden blessings of Psalm 24 and the seer anointing. Let's look at the passage in fullness and then we will look at it in detail a little later. I believe that as you read the coming pages you can have your life transformed by this revelation. Again, just believe to receive!

The earth is the Lord's, and all its fullness, The world and those who dwell therein. For He has founded it upon the seas, And established it upon the waters. Who may ascend into the hill of the Lord? Or who may stand in His holy place? He who has clean hands and a pure heart, Who has not lifted up his soul to an idol, Nor sworn deceitfully. He shall receive blessing from the Lord, and righteousness from the God of his salvation. This is Jacob, the generation of those who seek Him, Who seek Your face. Selah Lift up your heads, O you gates! And be lifted up, you everlasting doors! And the King of glory shall come in. Who is this King of glory? The Lord strong and mighty, The

LORD mighty in battle. Lift up your heads, O you gates! Lift up, you everlasting doors! And the King of glory shall come in. Who is this King of glory? The LORD of hosts, He is the King of glory. Selah* (Psalm 24:1-10).

The Lord has given me what I believe is some amazing and hidden revelation from this passage, and I want to share it all with you. However, I will also share several testimonies with you that the Lord has placed upon my heart to include in this book. We will look at those testimonies first. The Bible says in Revelation 19:10 that *"the testimony of Jesus is the spirit of prophecy."* I believe that the book in your hands right now contains the spirit of prophesy. In other words, this book represents an opportunity for you to step into these same kinds of supernatural experiences and angelic encounters. You can receive the same kinds of supernatural revelation depicted in this book from the Kingdom of Heaven in your life too.

One of the things we know at this hour is that our society has invested millions upon millions of dollars on studying the human body and developing ways we can heal the human body. We call that medicine and medical science. We've also invested millions upon millions of dollars on studying and developing ways to deal with the soul and issues of the soul. We call that psychology and other behavioral sciences. Even so, the human race, for the most part, has not advanced very much in reference to the study and development of the human spirit. But God wants us to understand and develop our human spirit because it is through our spirit that God relates to us. I pray that this book, in some small way, will help your spirit to become dominant in terms of your perception every day for the rest of your life. Amen

Think about this: if you live an additional ten years, that is only 3,650 days. Twenty years longer is only 7,300 days. My friend, redeem the time as the days are evil (Ephesians 5:16). But, I have some really good news for you! God can give you dominion over time when you learn to see and hear in a heavenly way. Time will no longer be your master, but time will be your slave! I touch on this supernatural exchange in the book *The Sword of the Lord and the Rest of the Lord*. But that is another message, so back to the issue at hand.

I want to share something that I believe the Lord has put upon my heart in reference to our spirit. I believe there is an opportunity for us today to have our spirit man become alive and more active than at any other time in history. We can see and hear things in the spiritual realm more easily today than we could even a year ago. I believe that a window has opened; I believe that a perpetual door has opened (Revelation 4:1; Deuteronomy 28:12). This is a heavenly door of grace and of God's supernatural favor. And anyone can walk through it into a new life and destiny. However, you must first be equipped to discern such a door in the heavenly realms. That is why we need to learn to have the seer anointing not only activated in our lives but also learn to walk in the seer realms as mature sons and daughters of the Most High God! I believe that there is openness in the heavenly realms that will allow us to see and hear what God is doing in our lives very clearly today. In my opinion, the graduation of Bob Jones was a spiritual signpost of this heavenly truth. Feb 14, 2014

One-on-one

We need to understand that we are all three-part beings, just like God is. In 1 Thessalonians 5:23, we find the Apostle Paul praying, *"Now may the God of peace Himself sanctify you completely; and may your whole spirit, soul, and body be preserved blameless at the coming of our Lord Jesus Christ."* You are reading this book to develop your spirit. If you want to read the book *Unlocking the Hidden Mysteries of the Seer Anointing*, there is a lot of teaching in there on how you can get your soul (mind, will, and emotions) sanctified and how you can bring your flesh into subjection to your spirit. But in this book I am going to take off to another level. So we know that we have three parts created just like the Trinity—God the Father, God the Son, and God the Holy Spirit. In this book I am going to focus on our spirit.

I am going to teach you the Word of God and then believe with you for impartation and activation of your inherent spiritual DNA and giftings. In the life and ministry of Jesus Christ, there were times when He came and immediately healed the sick. Yet, at other times Jesus taught principles from the Kingdom of Heaven before He ministered. That is what I am going to do: teach principles and share revelation from the Kingdom of Heaven from the word of God and then believe the Lord to release sovereign activation and to minister to you as an individual in a supernatural way! The Creator will minister to you, the creature, One-on-one.

I also believe that God will use the testimonies in this book according to the principle of Revelation 19:10; that the testimony of Jesus will be the spirit of prophesy for you as you read. Again, in my opinion, I believe that this book contains the spirit of prophesy for you! It is not necessary for me to be in the same room with you. In fact, I don't even have to be in the same nation with you, because God can sovereignly and supernaturally activate your spiritual vision and hearing. God Himself can release a spiritual blessing into your life and into your sphere of influence! You may even be reading this on an iPad, laptop, smart phone or some other digital device such as a Kindle Fire; but the Spirit can rest upon the digital words that you are reading! Just believe to receive it! There is no distance or limitations in the Spirit!

Prayer of Reception

Lord, I choose to believe to receive. Father, in Jesus' name, I purpose in my heart to believe to receive the prophetic promises that the Holy Spirit has placed into these pages. Lord, I am ready, I am willing, and I choose to receive everything that You are seeking to release to me from the Kingdom of Heaven though this book. Holy Spirit, I ask that You would guide me and teach me as I read the coming testimonies. Lord, I ask that You would open my spiritual eyes and activate my spiritual ears to see and hear in a Christlike way. Lord Jesus, You said that to me it has been given and granted to know the hidden mysteries of the Kingdom of Heaven. Today, Lord, I choose to revive those blessings and revelations that You have hidden for me in the Holy Scriptures. Help me to see the keys to unlock the hidden mysteries of Your word and of Your

Kingdom to me now. Lord, let Your Kingdom come into my life on earth as it is in heaven today. In the name of Jesus Christ of Nazareth I Pray. Amen!

CHAPTER 3

The Manifold Wisdom of Heaven

Let's look at 1 Corinthians 2:6 where Paul teaches us, "*We speak wisdom among those who are mature, yet not the wisdom of this age, nor of the rulers of this age, who are coming to nothing.*" This verse perfectly outlines what is happening right now on earth; there's a great shaking going on in the earth today. God is bringing the wisdom of man to nothing. However, at the same instant the Lord is preparing to release the manifold wisdom of Heaven to His friends.

Paul goes on to say in verse 7: "*But we speak the wisdom of God in a mystery, the hidden wisdom which God ordained before the ages for our glory.*" You see, God has hidden wisdom, hidden mysteries in His Kingdom He is releasing to us at this hour. He goes on in verses 8 and 9: "*Which none of the rulers of this age knew; for had they known, they would not have crucified the Lord of glory. But as it is written: 'Eye has not seen, nor ear heard, Nor have entered into the heart of man The things which God has prepared for those who love Him.'*"

These are keys here; that's the season we are stepping into. There are things that God has prepared for our eyes to see and our ears to hear that we cannot comprehend—not just yet. The key to unlocking this heavenly mystery is to love God. The key to going deeper in the seer anointing is to keep your spirit, soul, and body focused on the Lord Jesus Christ consistently, continuously without wavering. <u>The key to going deeper into the glory realms and operating in great power in the days to come is learning to cultivate the love of God in your life.</u> This, my friend, is not optional! I believe that you can have the strongest gifts of the Holy Spirit in your entire state or nation, <u>but if the gifts of the Spirit are not motivated by the love of</u> God they can lead you to sin at times. But, alas, that is another message too!

Spirit to spirit

Getting back to 1 Corinthians 2, in verse 10 we read, "*But God has revealed.*" What that language means is that God has made them visible; God is allowing us to see those things that our eyes have not seen. "*God has revealed them to us through His Spirit. For the Spirit searches all things, yes, the deep things of God.*" The hidden mysteries of the Kingdom of God are given to us by the Spirit. These hidden supernatural treasures are given Spirit to spirit. Do you want to unearth the deep things of God? Verse 11 tells us: "*For what man knows the things of a man except the spirit of the man which is in him? Even so no one knows the things of God except the Spirit of God.*" This is talking about hidden mysteries. This speaks of our inherent spiritual DNA to know heavenly mysteries!

Verse 12 continues, "*Now we have received, not the spirit of the world, but the Spirit who is from God.*" If we truly have the

Spirit of God, then the Spirit of God can reveal those hidden mysteries to us as we develop our spiritual eyes and ears. This supernatural spiritual enlightenment is the work of the Holy Spirit. The Holy Ghost imparts supernatural revelation and activates our ability to see and hear in a new way! This is Christ in you the hope of glory (Colossians 1:27)! This speaks of the Holy Spirit who's going to guide us and teach us. It is God's Spirit that is going to help us to step into these hidden mysteries. It is the Holy Spirit who is going to help us to develop our ability to see and to hear in a new and supernatural way! Thank You, Lord, for the Holy Ghost!

It's through our spirit man and our spiritual senses that the eyes of our understanding are going to see and our ears are going to hear. It is through our regenerated spirits that we are going to comprehend and discern these hidden mysteries of the Kingdom of God. Let's read it again so that it can soak deeply into our spirits: *"Now we have received, not the spirit of the world, but the Spirit who is from God, that we might **know** the things that have been freely given to us by God"* (1 Corinthians 2:12, emphasis added). Put your hand on your chest and say, "There are hidden and mysterious things that God has given to me freely. I can know hidden and mysterious revelation and wisdom from the Kingdom of Heaven. Amen!"

We read on in verse 13: *"These things we also speak, not in words which man's wisdom teaches but which the Holy Spirit teaches, comparing spiritual things with spiritual."*

Spiritual Discernment

Here's an important fact I want you to see and to understand. It says in verse 14: "*But the natural* [carnal, intellectual, fleshly] *man does not receive the things of the Spirit of God, for they are foolishness to him; nor can he know them, because they are spiritually discerned.*" I believe there is going to be an activation of supernatural spiritual discernment. You are going to have your ears open and your eyes open to see and hear things in a way that you've never seen and heard before.

The Lord is going to place upon you a supernatural grace for the spirit of wisdom and revelation to rest upon your life. You will begin to see and to hear from a heavenly perspective. Then you will not be subject to the plethora of ungodly doctrine and propaganda that is swirling around in the earthly or temporal realms. You will rise above the swirl to be seated with Christ in the heavenly places and from that position you will walk and live in victory! Hallelujah!

Paul also spoke of this type of supernatural revelation and wisdom in Ephesians 3: 8-11:

> *To me, who am less than the least of all the saints, this grace was given, that I should preach among the Gentiles the unsearchable riches of Christ, and to make all see what is the fellowship of the mystery, which from the beginning of the ages has been hidden in God who created all things through Jesus Christ; to the intent that now the manifold wisdom of God might be made known by the church to the principalities and powers in the*

heavenly places, according to the eternal purpose which He accomplished in Christ Jesus our Lord.

God intends for the manifold wisdom of heaven to be known through His friends to the powers of our day! There is clearly supernatural wisdom and revelation in the heavenly places that the Lord wishes to release to His friends at this hour. However, we need to learn to see and hear in a heavenly fashion. We need to get the revelation that we *can* be seated above the powers and principalities of the present evil age. You *can* be given keys to unlock the hidden mysteries and unsearchable riches of Christ at this hour!

I find that very exciting! As we continue with our search for these hidden mysteries, I believe that the King of Glory *will* release them to you as you press into the pages of this book! After all, Jesus promised us: *"I will give you the keys of the kingdom of heaven, and whatever you bind on earth will be bound in heaven, and whatever you loose on earth will be loosed in heaven"* (Matthew 16:19). In the next chapter we will begin to explore modern day testimonies of encounters with Jesus.

Prayer to Activate Godly Discernment

Lord, I ask You to reveal to me the secrets and hidden mysteries that eye has not seen nor ear heard. Lord, I ask You to ignite my heart by Your Spirit and let the Kingdom of heaven enter into my heart. Reveal to me the mysteries and the secret things that You have prepared for those who love You. I ask You, Father, in the name of Jesus, to reveal the fellowship of the mysteries and the unsearchable riches found in Christ to me. Reveal them to my spirit. O Lord, open my eyes to see the mysteries hidden in the Kingdom of Heaven. Lord, help me to discern the manifold wisdom of God. Lord I am asking You to give me eyes to see and ears to hear in a new and supernatural way. In the name of Jesus I pray. Amen!

CHAPTER 4

The Testimonies of Jesus

Now before we go back to Psalm 24 to discover the hidden mysteries and blessings there, I want to share the testimonies of Jesus from several experiences in my life. Over the last twelve years, the Lord has been speaking to me about the seer anointing. The first time it happened was on February 25, 2001; that's the day I fell down at an altar and received Jesus Christ as my Lord and Savior. The instant that happened, I was supernaturally delivered from a lifestyle of sin and drug addiction. For over thirty-one years I had been oppressed and struggled with these evil things. But in a moment and in a twinkle of an eye I was instantly delivered and set free from drug addiction. God Almighty began the process of transforming my character.

You need to understand that the Bible means exactly what is written in it. I was delivered from addiction to drugs instantly. I am no longer an addict. I am no longer an alcoholic. When I freely received the salvation of the Lord Jesus Christ, I received my freedom immediately. It was instantaneous. Let me encourage you that if you are battling addiction or other issues you can also be instantly delivered. The desire for the drugs lifted off of me instantaneously. "Hi, I am Kevin. I am a child of the Most High God!" Let me encourage you that you need to be careful with the words of your mouth. You are not an alcoholic. You are not a drug addict. If you choose to know Jesus Christ as your Lord and Savior, you can be recreated in an instant into a new creation! That literally happened to me, and it can literally happen to you.

Second Corinthians 5:17 makes this kind of supernatural transformation very clear: *"Therefore, if anyone is in Christ, he is a new creation; old things have passed away; behold, all things have become new."* If you have struggled in the past, remember that that battle is in the past and that all things have become new! Don't decree words over your life like: "Hi, I am John and I am a drug addict," or, "Hi, I am John and I am an alcoholic." In my opinion you will be what you decree. Be careful with the words of your mouth.

I have a little word decree that the Lord gave to me right after I was delivered from drug addiction. It goes like this: "I am truly blessed and highly favored with great, great grace and divine intervention in my life today. I am a King's kid and a royal priest according to the order of Melchizedek, and I am walking in the FOG (favor of God)." As I decreed this over my life, the Lord accelerated the transformation that was ongoing in my life. He took me from hopelessness to hope. He took me from poverty to prosperity. He took me from sickness to health.

Here is some good news for you: the Lord can do the same for you. Perhaps you might like to get my little testimonial book *31 Word Decrees That Will Revolutionize Your Life*. It works! We have seen dozens of heroin addicts, just like I was, instantly delivered and set free as I have prayed for them. I feel quickened by the Lord to pray for that now. If you are struggling with addiction and the desire to use drugs or engage in other nefarious things, pray this prayer of freedom.

Prayer of Freedom

Father, in the name of Jesus I choose to believe this testimony. Lord, the Bible tells us that You are no respecter of persons. What You did in Kevin's life You can do in my life. Lord, I confess that I am struggling with sin and addiction. I repent now and ask the Lord Jesus Christ to become the Lord of my life. Jesus, I ask that You would save me now and set me free from this addiction. Lord, deliver me from every demonic power and every generational curse associated with this addiction now. In Jesus' name, I command every demon of addiction to loose your assignment against my life right now. Addiction, go, in Jesus' name! Lord, I thank You for saving me and setting me free now. I choose to walk in the paths that You have chosen for me, Lord. And I choose to serve You and only You, Lord, all the days of my life. And Lord, I thank You for making me into a new creation with a new God-ordained destiny. Help me, Lord, to see and hear clearly from You today and every day. Amen.

The Work of the Spirit

Immediately after I prayed that simple prayer to receive Jesus as Savior on February 25, 2001, God began to open up my spiritual eyes and spiritual ears. (If you are not "born again" or do not know Jesus Christ as your Lord and Savior, you can pray the prayer of salvation in the Table of Prayers near the end of this book). The Creator of the heavens and the earth began the process of speaking to me in many different ways. Please notice that I said "process." Learning to hear and to see the things of God can be an ongoing process and learning curve. Just purpose in your heart not to give up and keep pressing into the Kingdom of God diligently.

Over the course of the next three weeks, I developed an insatiable hunger for the word of God. In hindsight I know now that this was the gentle work of the Holy Spirit. The night that I prayed to receive Jesus as Lord and Savior I was given an old King James Bible. That Bible has been around the world with me many times as of this writing. As I read the scriptures, I saw where this Man named Jesus Christ fasted and prayed. So, led by the Spirit of God, I also began to fast and pray. I mean, if it was good enough for Jesus, it must be good enough for me, right? God was listening, and He was also paying attention! Today I know that Jesus was actually sitting at the right hand of the Father praying for me (Hebrews 7:25). In fact, the Lord Jesus is also praying for you right now, even as you read this.

On the night of March 13, 2001, I had the first of many encounters with God. It was 1:13 a.m. and the heavens seemed to open up. I had been reading the old King James Bible and praying. I remember telling the Lord that if He was real then I wanted to see Him! But, if He was like many of the people that I was seeing in the church, I did not want anything to do with

Him or this so-called Christianity. I fell into a sound sleep with that heartfelt prayer on my lips.

Sometime later I awoke with a start to the pungent smell of roses and honey, and what I now know as the glory of God was hanging heavily in the air. A reverential fear percolated up from somewhere deep within my spirit. It seemed that the room was now glowing faintly and every hair on my body seemed to be standing at attention. I am not sure, but I believe that at that moment Jesus Christ stepped into my brother's little living room. I sensed that the Lord was flanked by angels, innumerable angels. This is part of the seer anointing; this is an aspect of our ears hearing and our eyes seeing things that we have not known. God wants you to experience these types of supernatural encounters too.

I was instructed to "reach out" to the youth of the small town that I was living in. God instructed me, giving me a plan for evangelism. That night the King of Glory Christian Music Festival was born in the glory realms. Jesus spoke to me and promised me that if I would be obedient to His instructions, I would see one hundred and twenty young people saved in less than one hundred and twenty days. At one point I asked the Lord to stop speaking to me for a moment. I was getting too much revelation, and I asked if He would wait until I could get a pencil and paper to write it all down. Because of this supernatural encounter I began to reach out to the lost in my city through the King of Glory Christian Music Festival. I can point to that night as the beginning of my ability to discern and perceive angelic activity.

I wrote down the very detailed instructions that were being spoken to me in the glory. During this amazing supernatural encounter, the Lord began to drop scriptures into my heart. The first passage that the Lord gave to me was Psalm 24. He told me to meditate upon it and to base the coming outreach on this passage. By the way, I witnessed one hundred and twenty-eight young people pray to receive Jesus Christ as Lord and Savior within one hundred and twenty days.

That was the origins of the name of the King of Glory Christian Music Festival, and that is how the ministry was born. I have read and reread the scriptures from Psalm 24 over and over for years. Yet, I was not aware of the awesome and supernatural blessings and promises that are contained in that Psalm of David. In the next chapter I will begin to share some of the supernatural testimonies and angelic visitations that helped to launch me further into experiencing and discerning the Kingdom of Heaven.

CHAPTER 5

Blessed Indeed!

Something else rather amazing started to happen that night. When the Lord stepped into that little room, He was accompanied by numerous heavenly angelic beings. Although I did not see these heavenly messengers on March 13th, I was certainly aware of their presence and the power of God that emanated from them.

Another supernatural manifestation also of the Kingdom of Heaven was activated in my life at this time. I began to smell the fragrances of frankincense and myrrh permeate the atmosphere of the room. This supernatural visitation lasted for what seemed like an eternity. However, in the natural realm it was about forty-five minutes. Once I had finished writing down the instructions that the Lord was giving to me, I relaxed for a moment imbibing the wonderful fragrance, presence, and glory of God that was hovering in the room. In fact, even today these heavenly fragrances manifest frequently as I am preaching and ministering. The scriptures describe manifestations of Christ's Kingdom like these as signs and wonders (Acts 4:30).

The Lord told me that the ministry must be based upon Psalm 24 and that He would give me more revelation as to the importance of this in the future. As a new believer I was expecting this revelation to come in the next few days. In fact, when the Lord finally released an additional portion of this promised revelation, more than twelve years had passed. I had been supernaturally launched into international ministry. By the unmerited grace of God, I had been released and empowered to travel to thirty-six nations to preach the Gospel of the Kingdom. I have witnessed tens of thousands of people pray to receive Jesus Christ as Lord and Savior in our meetings. We have witnessed every miracle that is outlined in the Bible as we have preached the word of God with signs and wonders accompanying the message of the Cross (Mark 16:20). To God be all the glory, all of the honor, and all of the praise!

Above All That I Could Think, Ask, or Imagine

On March 13, 2001, I could never have imagined that it would take twelve years for this promised revelation to come! Nor could I fathom how the Lord would move and open up the supernatural grace and favor upon my life and the ministry the Lord birthed that night. You see, the King of Glory Christian Music Festival later became King of Glory Ministries International in April 2004. In fact, as I was filling out the forms to establish the ministry, the same presence, fragrances, and glory of God invaded my space in Kansas City, Missouri. I sat there weeping at the goodness and nearness of the Lord. I was just about to fill in the space on the form that would establish the ministry's name.

I had just finished writing the letter "y" in "glory" when the glory fell and the fragrance of Jesus filled my little office at 11200 Kensington Avenue. Jesus spoke to me in what may have well been an audible voice saying, "International." At that instant I had the understanding that the ministry was to be called King of Glory Ministries International. A few years later in 2007 I came to the realization that we had ministered internationally about 95 percent of the time; very rarely did we speak and preach in the USA.

Jabez

This is what I like to refer to as a "teachable moment." One *legitimate* word from the Lord can transform your destiny in an instant. That is why it is so crucial to learn to discern the voice of the Lord at this hour.

Going back to March 13, 2001, I knew that I needed to "do something." The first thing that I did was to begin to recruit people who the Lord had shown me to begin to pray the "prayer of Jabez" in agreement with me. That prayer is found in 1 Chronicles 4:9-10:

> *Now Jabez was more honorable than his brothers, and his mother called his name Jabez, saying, "Because I bore him in pain." And Jabez called on the God of Israel saying, "Oh, that You would bless me indeed, and enlarge my territory, that Your hand would be with me, and that You would keep me from evil, that I may not cause pain!" So God granted him what he requested.*

As the Lord instructed, I began to pray the prayer of Jabez without ceasing! I would just tailor the prayer to every need that would come up as I sought to prepare for King of Glory Christian Music Festival. The Lord began to move the mountains in my life and every obstacle to orchestrating a music festival. In short order, the Lord provided the venue. It was the Sarah Creasy Metcalf Amphitheater in Bluefield, Virginia.

The sound system for the event was procured. We received underwriting for advertising on the radio. The Lord provided funds for free food and other forms of advertising. This encounter created a hunger for God in my life, and the Lord began to open the realms of the supernatural to me. Because of this hunger for God, I fasted and read the Bible voraciously during this season.

Frankincense and Myrrh

I began to experience the realms of glory and the Lord's angels as the "fragrance" of the Lord would invade my time and space. During this amazing season there was an abundance of angelic activity unfolding around me in a very consistent way. The grace and favor of the Lord manifested in my life. A lot of folks began to recognize that God was answering my prayers in supernatural ways. "Natural miracles" became common in my life. One of those "natural miracles" was the donation of a large banner for the festival. The banner reads "Jesus King of Glory" in bold red letters. On the night of August 22, 2001, I took the new banner to the church and asked the pastor if we could pray over it, anoint it, and prepare it for Kingdom use.

He agreed. The church gathered around the new banner. I was on the left side. I spread the new banner out in front of the altar and the saints began to pray over it, anointing it with oil. As of today that banner has been witness to tens of thousands of salvations. I closed my eyes and began to pray reverently in the Holy Spirit. Instantly the familiar fragrances of the heavenly realms began to envelop me. Soon I felt a pair of very gentle yet strong hands resting upon my shoulders. The hands were very large and very warm; you could say that these were anointed hands!

At that instant I felt the sensation of warm oil being poured over my head. I wondered if they were actually pouring the whole bottle of anointing oil from the altar on me. I had the impression of oil flowing along my entire back and chest. As this heavenly oil flowed, there was an increase of the fragrance of frankincense and myrrh. The tangible glory of God began to course through my spirit, soul, and somewhat tired body. I was thinking to myself, "Who on earth is this that is praying for me." I had never had such an anointed person pray for me like this before. I could feel that there was power and great authority in those supernatural hands.

I'm not sure how long I was resting in the glory there on my knees with my hands on the banner praying in the Holy Spirit. All the while those heavenly hands rested upon my shoulders and there seemed to be an impartation that was taking place the whole time. After a long time I opened my eyes and looked around. I realized that the other people had returned to their designated spots on the hard wooden pews.

Remaining upon my knees with my hands upon the left edge of the new banner, I could still tangibly feel those large warm hands resting upon my back. I thought, "Praise the Lord; someone stood beside me while I prayed." I stood up to thank that "person," and quickly turned around to see who was praying for me. I was shocked to find that there was no one there! There was no one in proximity to me at all. I was totally stunned! Just an instant before those large hands were resting upon my shoulders and I had also discerned a soft voice praying in a heavenly language along with me. The voice was clear and prayed into my left ear. I gathered up the banner and weaved back to my seat under the influence of the Holy Spirit. The wonderful anointing and the abiding glory of God rested upon me for weeks!

This supernatural encounter seemed to release a divinely ordained increase of the grace and favor that God was placing upon my life in this season. Later I returned to my little house at 121 Beech Street and immediately went into my little prayer room. I wept bitterly (yet they were tears of true joy). I began to call out to the Lord and give Him thanks. I sought to give the Lord all of the honor and all of the praise for this amazing supernatural encounter. I knew the Father had sent a mighty angel to minister to me and to strengthen my resolve that night. The truth is that I needed to be strengthened for the work that I had been commissioned to complete.

As I prayed to the Lord, I began to ask Him why this had transpired. *"Lord, what was happening as I felt that fragrant warm oil running down my head and body?"* Instantly the Spirit of God reminded me of the words that I had been praying with fasting for weeks: *"Oh that You would bless me indeed, and that Your hand would be upon me"* (1 Chronicles 4:10).

I believe that God Almighty had released one of His angels from the heavenly realms to place his hands upon me! Perhaps the angel released an anointing and gift of grace upon my life at the Lord's instruction. After that night I had an unshakable revelation that God's angels are an important part of His Kingdom. The Lord definitely uses His angelic host to minister to His people. In my opinion, the Lord had actually assigned this angel to minister and help me.

I have never believed that Godly angelic visitations were scary, spooky, or unnatural. The scriptures are replete with the ministry of angels. And if angelic ministry is in the word of God, I choose to accept them without hesitation. I simply embraced angelic ministry with childlike faith. After all, this angelic encounter is still bearing fruit today!

In fact, everything came together in a divine and supernatural way. On Friday August 31, 2001, King of Glory Christian Music Festival went off without a hitch. People were saved, healed, delivered, and set free. I write about these amazing miraculous events in more detail in the first book of the trilogy, *The Reality of Angelic Ministry Today: How to Work with the Angels in Your Life.*

A Prayer Modeled After Jabez

O Lord, I ask that You would bless me indeed. Lord, I am asking that You would expand my territory and allow me to hear and to see in new and heavenly ways. O Lord, that You would place Your mighty right hand upon me and strengthen me to walk in the paths that You have preordained for me to walk in. O Lord, that You would bless me in a great and mighty way. And Father, I ask in Jesus' name that I might not be the cause of any pain. In the mighty name of Jesus I pray. Amen.

Let me conclude this chapter by saying that the Lord is about the business of raising up "suddenlies" at this hour. Jesus will save and deliver people from gross sin and, like me, decades of addiction and launch them out into the great harvest overnight. This testimony is a prophetic promise for you. It is not too late for you. It is not too late for your family. That child, grandson, or daughter can be saved and changed in an instant and in a twinkle of an eye. Don't stop praying for their salvation and total transformation. I know by revelation that it was the prayers of my grandmother, Lula May Burnopp, that changed my life.

In fact, the Lord showed this to me in a vision. I saw my grandmother lift me up to the Lord in her hands and commit my life to Him. That was in 1959. Forty-one years later, God in His sovereignty, released the answer to those prayers of Grandma Lula May Burnopp. Never give up. Never stop praying for God to move the mountains that are in your life and in your family. He is the God of the impossible! In the next chapter I will share some testimonies about how violently seeking the Kingdom of Heaven can unlock the doors of supernatural provision and transform your life. In fact, the Creator of Heaven and Earth may even reveal Himself to you!

Prayer of Transformation

Lord, Your word teaches that if anyone is in Christ he becomes a new creation. Lord, I choose to commit my ways to You right now. I choose to be in Christ. And Father, I am asking You to release and activate a supernatural transformation in my life and circumstances. Lord, take me from the darkness and translate me into the Kingdom of Your Son and into Your Kingdom of Light. Ignite a supernatural transformation in my life and set a heavenly fire deep down in my soul. Transform me into the very image of Your beloved Son, Jesus. Lord, help me to see the reality of Your Kingdom and step into the fullness of the destiny that You have prepared for me. In Jesus' name I pray. Amen!

CHAPTER 6

The Metamorphosis of a Life

Because of these supernatural experiences I began to develop a desperate hunger for more of the Lord. I had an insatiable appetite to enter into the reality of the Kingdom of God. I did not want religion or a form of God. I wanted the *real thing* or nothing at all! If this thing called Christianity was true, I was desperate for the God of heaven and earth to reveal Himself to me! What is more, I began to ask the Lord for this in a consistent and ongoing way. The Lord was apparently listening to my prayers and started to move on my behalf.

Jesus started a metamorphosis in my life. During this period I moved into a season of extended prayer and fasting. When the King of Glory Christian Music Festival concluded, the grace and favor that had been upon my life seemed to vanish. I was still experiencing the manifest presence of the Lord during times of prayer; however, the fragrance and anointing of God would fill my prayer room at 121 Beech Street, Bluefield, West Virginia, less frequently. Much to my dismay, the manifestations of God's presence had decreased greatly too. This perplexed me. *after the 80's*

I began to get desperate for God. In hindsight I believe that the Holy Spirit orchestrated and initiated my supernatural thirst. I was concerned about not discerning the presence of God as I had before the festival. So I began to press into God all the more. At times I would sequester myself in the little house and fast and pray for up to seven days until the tangible glory of God would fall. I sensed that the Lord had another assignment for me to uncover. I felt in my spirit that the Lord was going to do another "<u>new thing" in my life. This "knowing" gave me a bit of an unsettling feeling. Nonetheless, I began to ask the Lord what the next assignment would be</u>. It was during these times of prayer the Lord began to speak to me about traveling to Newfoundland. Deep within my spirit I understood that the Lord was about to stretch me. Perhaps you also have an unsettling feeling like this within your spirit at this time?

Snorkeling With Jesus or the Bully Pulpit

It was during this period of violently seeking the Lord that the Holy Spirit began to nudge me. His Spirit was leading me to travel to Newfoundland, Canada. It was during October of 2001 when the Lord began to speak to me about Newfoundland. I had no desire to go there, especially in the middle of the winter! I had been getting "beat up" in the church for the work I had done for the King of Glory Christian Music Festival. So I had purposed in my heart to go to St. John in the Virgin Islands. Yes, that was a good idea! Just me and Jesus snorkeling with the tropical fish. I could escape the bully pulpit and get away from that religious spirit that seemed to take great pride and zeal in tormenting me! Yes, St. John sounded warm and inviting! Surely this was the Lord. I began to investigate the logistics and costs to take my Caribbean snorkeling tour with the Lord.

However, it seemed that God had another idea. Yes, He wanted me to go to St. John, but the St. John that the Lord had in mind was in the Great White North; St John's Newfoundland! I recall debating with the Holy Spirit on this point. Do you ever argue with the Spirit of God? Well, here is a news flash for you: you cannot win that argument. I remember the conversation well. "Lord, You know that Newfoundland is really cold in November?" All that I heard in response was silence.

"Lord, You know that we would have a much better time at Cinnamon Bay snorkeling and fellowshipping together, right?" Again, silence. "Lord, you know that it would be much warmer on St. John. We could really have a wonderful time together; You could speak to me and we could dive into the crystal clear waters together. It would be great fun!" Again, silence.

It began to dawn upon my spirit that the Lord had another plan that He wanted to enact, and silently within my spirit I knew that the trip to the Caribbean was not going to happen in the winter of 2001. But, just maybe, God would change His mind!

That's the devil

It was at this time that an abundance of signs were given to me to make the trip to St. John's, Newfoundland! The only person that I knew in Newfoundland called me and said something like this: "Kevin, the Lord spoke to me in prayer this morning. I think that you are supposed to come to Newfoundland for some upcoming revival meetings here." I remember my first thought: "That is the devil! I am going to St. John in the Virgin Islands!" Later that day I stopped off at my mother's home to visit with her. She was watching a Public Broadcasting Service special. In fact, she said, "Kevin, I think you should watch this with me. It is really interesting." The program was about Newfoundland! Mom did not know that internal struggle that I was wrestling with! "Mom, I just remembered that I need to go somewhere." Out the door I went, arguing with the Spirit of God again! A few days later I received a post card from Newfoundland!

Holding the post card in my hand, I stepped up the heat in my ongoing debate with the Lord. I was sure that I was supposed to go to St. John in the Virgin Islands. I was equally sure that the devil was seeking to trick me into going to Newfoundland in the middle of an arctic winter. I hate the cold, but I love to snorkel! "Lord, if this is You who is leading me to go to Canada, then you will have to make a way. Lord, You know that I do not have enough money for an airline ticket to Newfoundland."

The Spirit of God said, "Check the price of the tickets." I thought to myself, "OK, Lord, I will look as soon as I leave here." As it turned out the price of the tickets was extremely low; perhaps because of the events of 9/11/2001. I actually had the money with two more dollars in my account than the cost of the airline tickets to Newfoundland. Canada, here I come! Sometimes God gives you "just enough" and you must move out in both faith and obedience. Once you take the first step of faith, He will meet you and supply your needs along the supernatural paths that He has ordained for you. (See Genesis 22:13-14; Psalm 119:105.)

So after many confirmations in the spirit, I pooled all of my earthly wealth and made the trip to the Great White North. The night before I was to depart the Lord instructed me to "pray in tongues all the way to Newfoundland." Somehow, through the grace of God, I succeeded in praying in the Spirit for about eighteen hours until I touched down in Newfoundland, Canada. Little did I know how simple obedience to be in the right place at the right time would open up the windows and doors of heaven over my life and circumstances. I call this chronological and geographical obedience, and I have written extensively about this spiritual principle in the first book of the seer trilogy. In the next chapter I share the testimony of how the Lord activated and accelerated the seer anointing in my life.

Prayer for Geographical Obedience

Father, by You all things both in heaven and upon earth were created. Lord, You created time. And at this time, Father, I ask You, in the might Name of Jesus Christ of Nazareth, to give me favor with time. Lord, I ask that I would discern the times and seasons in my life. Help me to have supernatural revelation each day of Your perfect timing in my life. Help me to be geographically and chronologically obedient to Your Spirit. Lord, give me revelation and show me where I should be and when I should be there. Help me to know, without doubt or shadow of wavering, what is Your good, acceptable, and the perfect will for my life. And Lord, help me to walk in Your perfect timing in all things. Father, You give wisdom to the wise and knowledge to those who have understanding; and I ask You, O Lord, to bless me with understanding of the times and seasons of heaven for my life right now. In Jesus name I pray. Amen.

CHAPTER 7

A New Found Land

In Springdale, Newfoundland, Canada, the Lord began instructing me to complete a series of prophetic actions. I attended an intercessory prayer meeting on Wednesday, November 21st. We were interceding for an upcoming series of healing meetings. During this meeting I began to "see" into the spirit. As the Lord opened my spiritual eyes, I incrementally saw the heavens open over Living Waters Ministries church.

In addition to this, I also began to hear angelic voices singing along with the worship team. At one point during the meeting, I saw a stream of golden oil pour out from heaven and land upon a certain spot in the sanctuary. At the leading of the Lord, I knelt upon that spot. The glory and anointing began to flow into and over my body. The sensation and anointing was very similar to what I experienced when the angel put his hands upon me the night of August 22, 2001. I was beginning to see and hear in a new way.

As I knelt under the spot where the golden oil was pouring onto the altar out of heaven, I was praying earnestly. I could feel the liquid oil raining down on my body. I could sense and smell this heavenly oil as it rolled off of my head. The Holy Spirit began to talk to me in a very clear and direct way which I had never experienced before. I collapsed onto the carpet in a pool of this golden oil and a puddle of tears. I lay there in the anointing of the Holy Spirit and the intense glory of God for what seemed like hours.

The Holy Spirit commenced to work within and upon me to spark a supernatural transformation. Today I understand that this transformation would not have been able to transpire at Cinnamon Bay, St. John. I was in the right place at the right time. You could call this the fruit of obedience. Abraham came to such a place in Genesis 22 when the Lord opened the windows and doors of heaven over his life and spoke blessings over him and his progeny. The Lord is still Jehovah-Jireh, or Yahovah Yireh. We find this encounter in Genesis 22:15-18:

> *The Angel of the LORD called to Abraham a second time out of heaven, and said: "By Myself I have sworn, says the LORD, because you have done this thing, and have not withheld your son, your only son—blessing I will bless you, and multiplying I will multiply your descendants as the stars of the heaven and as the sand which is on the seashore; and your descendants shall possess the gate of their enemies. In your seed all the nations of the earth shall be blessed, because you have obeyed My voice."*

In my geographical place of blessing, I began to sense angels dancing all around the supernatural pool of golden oil and glory. The angels of the Lord seemed to be dancing all around me too. I felt an angel as it brushed its wings across my face.

I had a "knowing" that the angel was asking me to raise my hands into the air. When I would raise my hands up to about two feet, the angel would push my hands back down with its strong warm hands. I would try again and I would almost get my hands totally up and the angel would tickle my nose with the feathers of its wings.

I would laugh and my hands would fall to the ground. The angel and I continued to interact in this fashion for nearly an hour. I did not actually see this angel, but the force and reality of its tactile touch was very tangible. There was no doubt that I was interacting with a heavenly being. Perhaps I was being trained to lift my hands into the glory realms? This experience seemed to help open up my spiritual senses to a much greater level than I had ever experienced up to that time. I suppose that you could accurately say I entered into a supernatural season of impartation and activation of my God inherent spiritual DNA. The transformation initiated by my obedience and the Spirit of God accelerated.

Tiny White Feathers

On Thursday, November 22nd, the healing meetings started. In these meetings God began to open my spiritual eyes beyond anything I could have ever imagined. On the first night of these meetings, I began to see an "open heaven" forming in the sanctuary. I could also hear and sense the activity of angels as the "heavens" continued to "open up" to a greater degree. On Friday the 23rd I began to see "bolts of light" shoot through the church and again the stream of golden oil was flowing from the open heaven in a greater volume onto a certain spot on the carpet. On Saturday night the 24th during the worship service, I began to see delicate tiny white feathers falling freely around the church and again began to hear the voices of angels singing very clearly in the natural realm. I was astonished at this new-found sensitivity.

Let me take just a moment to speak of these delicate tiny white feathers. I have discovered that there is a segment of people out there who become offended by this manifestation of the Kingdom of Heaven. You see, I still have this type of sign and wonder transpire around me on a consistent basis. Angels feathers (yes, I said angels feathers) will begin to appear mid-air and float around my head at times. There have been many people who have witnessed this phenomenon over the years. Many times as I am writing, these delicate little "kisses from heaven" will begin to flutter around my head. In fact, angels' feathers started to float around my head as I was writing this today! Why? Well, by who's authority do you ask, "Why?" My answer to you is: "Why not?" To me it is obvious that God's angels are active when these little gifts from Heaven appear. Perhaps we would be better off just to look to the One who releases such signs and wonders; focus upon the Giver of the gift and not the gift, per se. That now concludes my mini sermon on angels' feathers.

Intense and Tangible Glory

As the worship proceeded that evening, I began to feel the tangible and intense glory of God flood the room. I was worshiping Jesus with all of my heart near the front row. Suddenly I felt like I should open my eyes and look at the worship team.

I was hearing dozens of singers accompanying the small worship team consisting of only five or six individuals. I was certain that angels were singing in unison with them. When I opened my eyes, I saw the source of the increased glory. Rose and Colleen had one hand raised and one hand upon a microphone as they were singing. When I glanced behind them I saw a man adorned in a white robe standing there. His robe was immaculate. It was whiter than any garment I have seen on earth and seemed to give off a translucent glow. (See Matthew 17:2; Luke 24:4.)

At first I shook my head and blinked my eyes thinking that they were playing a trick on me. When I opened my eyes again, this mighty angel of God was still there. I leaned forward and really strained my eyes for a good look. This impressive angel was looking me right in the eyes. This magnificent angel was gazing at me! The angel gave me a big smile and then he winked at me! My mouth dropped open and my eyes budged out as every hair on my body stood on end! He continued to smile at me and look me over. Again I blinked my eyes and tried to shake off this vision that was so crystal clear to me. Again when I opened my eyes this angel was still there. He was still smiling at me and standing in a posture of attention and readiness. The angel continued to inspect me from head to toe. This was a bit unnerving having never encountered such an angel before for such an extended segment of time. The material of his robe looked phosphorescent. I was stunned.

This heavenly visitor stood about twelve feet tall. He had long golden hair about shoulder length. His eyes were a bright piercing blue. He had a golden belt or sash around his waist.

Upon the sash was a large two-edged sword with a heavy golden handle. On his wrists were ornate golden bands, and his feet were clad with golden sandals. He also carried a large golden shield that was of the finest workmanship. I watched this angel throughout the entire worship service. The angel would look at different individuals in the sanctuary from time to time. I was totally engrossed in observing every aspect of him. I was mesmerized by what I was witnessing. Every so often he would glance at me and offer another smile.

The momentum of these healing meetings continued to build. In desperation I positioned my heart to encounter God. I continued to see the "open heaven" swirling in the sanctuary of Living Waters Ministries. I was still seeing feathers, bolts of lightning, and hearing dozens of angels singing along with the worship team. Saturday evening, November 24th, the "open heaven" had grown to about twenty-five feet in circumference. I was well able to see it with my natural eyes and continued to watch it spin over the church.

I was praying and observing everything. I was lying prostrate on the floor unable to move my body. I could see and I could hear but was totally unable to move. It was as if I was "glued' to the floor. However, I kept my eyes focused upon the "open heaven" that was swirling in the church. The Lord had started to accelerate the process of activating my spirit to see and hear in a new way. However, I was totally unprepared for what happened next.

CHAPTER 8

Greater Glory

On Sunday morning, November 25, 2001, in that little city called Springdale, I saw the heavens open up once more to a greater degree. The pastor asked Dean to share his testimony about seeing Jesus. Dean was unable to speak because he was weeping intensely. As I lay there on the floor, I was observing the portal or open heaven that had now grown to be about forty-five feet in circumference.

Once more there was a flurry of activity around the edge of the open heaven as I found myself in the same position on Sunday evening. The young man named Dean stood up to give a testimony about seeing Jesus step into the church in the Saturday evening service. Dean was totally undone and unable to speak about his experience. When he began to share, there was a flurry of activity around the edge of the "open heaven," which I was monitoring from my horizontal position on the floor. Several angels scurried to the edge and began to excitedly talk among themselves and point down at Dean. Angels of every shape and size leaned over the edge to see and hear what Dean was about to say. Once more the intense tangible glory of God began to rain down upon me as I was on the floor. At first there were only about six angels around the opening. Quickly more of God's angels began to peer over the edge of the portal, and they were very keen to hear and see what was transpiring in the sanctuary. Soon a plethora of angels began to fill the circumference of the portal.

There appeared to be angels of all ages, shapes, and sizes. I saw several small angels that appeared to be young children. (Jesus Himself referred to these in Matthew 18:10.) I also witnessed angels that appeared to be adults. There were also other smaller angels that were holding musical instruments. These instruments had the aspects of horns and trumpets and others looked like flutes or reed instruments. There was a varied and vast assortment of angels represented in the small group of about forty-five heavenly beings. I watched these angels for the rest of the service. Soon I began to realize that the angels were aware of the fact that I could see them. Many of them began to point in my direction and to speak to one another animatedly. This was fascinating. It seemed that the group of the angels were also fascinated that I was able to see and discern them too.

A Band of Angels

The angels around the open heaven were all speaking to one another excitedly. They seemed to be having a great time. The angels were pointing to different people and many were singing and playing small stringed instruments! I was enamored by what I was seeing and hearing. In addition to this, because of the intense glory I was glued to the floor, unable to move my body save for a finger or two and my eyes. Suddenly I saw a section of the portal open up and the angels that were positioned around the entire circumference of the open heaven shifted. That is when I saw the large powerful angelic being that I had seen in the worship a couple of nights before step up to the edge of the opening and speak in a language that I did not understand.

Immediately the other angels seemed to become more orderly and reverent. They stopped their laughter and animated behavior. This band of angels then turned to look back behind the larger angelic being. I watched as he stepped back. Then I saw Him. Jesus stepped up to the edge of the portal and held out His hands. The Lord Jesus was now standing at the edge of the opening, and He seemed to be pouring out what appeared to be gemstones into the service. I could see and hear as diamonds, rubies, sapphires, and pearls seemed to hit the carpet and bound around me. I thought, "It doesn't get any better than this." The tangible glory of God was incredible at that moment. In case you are wondering, I did look for those heavenly gemstones.

Suddenly Jesus took a step with His right foot and descended into the service. He moved over to stand behind Dean as he was sharing his testimony about seeing Jesus. Remember, the testimony of Jesus is the spirit of prophecy (Revelation 9:10)! When Jesus entered the service, time seemed to stand still and the unsearchable love of Christ began to wash over me in waves. It seemed that the tangible glory of the Lord increased even more. Suddenly I was overcome by the fragrances of roses, cinnamon, frankincense, myrrh, and honey. These beautiful aromas fused into what I now understand to be the fragrance of the Lord.

A Whole New Dimension

I was undone as I cast my gaze upon Jesus! I thought once more, "It doesn't get any better than this." This was in fact the answer to the prayer that I had been praying constantly every day for the past several months. It turned out to be a dangerous prayer. Yes, that was it! I prayed to be like that guy Saul. I had been telling the Lord: "Jesus, if You are real, then I want You to come and visit me. I want to be knocked off of my horse. I want you to appear to me like You appeared to that dude Saul. Show me a light from heaven! I want to get up from the ground picking gravel from my teeth. Then you can send some guy like Ananias to come and lay his hands upon me to receive my sight and the Holy Spirit. Yeah! That is what I want, Jesus; You just come and reveal yourself to me!" (I suppose, in hindsight, I was unwittingly asking the Lord to help me to see and hear in new ways through my dangerous prayers!)

As I lay there thinking, "It doesn't get any better than this," it occurred to me that Jesus was answering those zealous prayers at that instant. I continued to look intently at the Lord. He now had His hands on Dean's shoulders and was searching the sanctuary with His eyes. I watched as the Lord moved His eyes from the right to the left. It seemed that He was searching the hearts of the men and women who were present (Jeremiah 17:10). The Lord looked over His flock for several minutes. All the while I was resting in the most powerful presence and glory of God that I have ever experienced. Waves and billow after billow of God's love washed over me like the tide of a beach. After a time Jesus turned and focused His gaze upon me. I melted.

I experienced the love of Christ in a whole new dimension. As the Lord looked into my heart and looked directly into my eyes, I was undone. I was undone by His love and the fact that He died for me! I thought, "It doesn't get any better than this!" Then the Lord took His hands off of Dean's shoulders and began to walk towards me.

The tangible glory and power multiplied exponentially with each step that He took. Finally, Jesus came and stood directly over me with one foot on each side of my body. He smiled. The love of God totally engulfed me at that instant. I gazed into the beautiful eyes of Jesus. He has the most beautiful eyes in the universe. The Lord's eyes are like two crystal blue pools of mercy and grace. I thought to myself again, "It does not get any better than this!"

Then Jesus spoke to me as a man speaks to his friend. (See Exodus 33:11.)

Dangerous Prayer

Lord, if You are real, then I want to see You. I want to experience Your love and glory first hand. Lord, I want to be like that guy called Saul in Acts 9. Yes, Lord! Let a light from heaven shine upon me! Jesus, come and speak to me Face-to-face, like a man does to a friend. Jesus, if You are real, then I want You to come and visit me. I want to be knocked off of my horse. I want you to appear to me like

You appeared to that dude Saul. Show me a light from heaven! Reveal Yourself to me, Jesus. Let me be knocked off of my high horse! Let me have to get up from the road picking gravel from between my teeth. Lord, anoint and empower some guy like Ananias to come and lay his hands upon me that I might may receive my sight and have my spiritual vision activated! O Lord, that I might be filled with the fullness of Your Holy Spirit. Open my eyes to see You, Lord Jesus. Open my ears to hear You speak to me, my God! Help me to see and hear in a new and supernatural way. In Jesus name I pray. Amen!

CHAPTER 9

Who Is the Messiah?

The Lord Jesus bent down and His face was now only two or three feet from mine. I could see His face perfectly, and I was mesmerized by His eyes of compassion and love. The glory of God seemed to radiate from His smile. I was now totally undone. I could not think. All that I was able to do was to imbibe His glory and become imbued with the love of Jesus as He stood over me. Again, I realized that the Lord had come to me in answer to my dangerous prayer to be like Saul. Then Jesus spoke to me very gently.

> He said, "All authority has been given to Me in heaven and on earth. Go therefore and make disciples of all the nations, baptizing them in the name of the Father and of the Son and of the Holy Spirit, teaching them to observe all things that I have commanded you; and lo, I am with you always, even to the end of the age. For I know the thoughts that I think toward you. My thoughts for you are thoughts for your good to give you a future and a hope. And you will seek Me and find Me, when you

search for Me with all your heart" (Matthew 28:18-20; Jeremiah 29:11-13).

After He spoke these things, Jesus continued to linger over me. I continued to absorb His love and glory. In fact, I believe that the glory of God is His love. I continued to gaze into the eyes of the Messiah. It is true that He was sent to be the Savior for every tongue, every tribe, and every nation. Elohim sent Jesus, Yeshua, to be Messiah for both Jew and Gentile. Revelation of this fact coursed supernaturally though my spirit. *I was* totally frozen by the proximity of the Lord Jesus Christ of Nazareth. I was unable to move or to think, but I understood that Jesus wanted me to lift my left hand. Perhaps that was why the angel had helped me to exercise my hands in the glory previously? Somehow I raised my hand and was surprised when Jesus took my hand gently in His hands. I could see the nail scars there, I could feel the wounds. This made me want to weep, but in His presence I was unable to shed a single tear. At that instant a thought bubbled up from somewhere: "It doesn't get any better than this!"

In the Twinkle of an Eye

Jesus held my hand as He looked deeply into my eyes for a couple of moments. The love and the glory of God that was resting upon me at that instant were incredible. It seemed that oil was flowing from my hand down my arm and dripping off of my elbow. I could smell the glory of God now, and I could sense the fragrance of the oil. After a moment the Lord breathed upon my hand and then He kissed it before laying it gently back upon my chest. I thought, "It doesn't get any better than this!" Jesus lingered over me for several minutes. I could have asked Him about anything, but it seemed that my mind was totally absorbed with Him. My lips were frozen by the proximity of the Lord Jesus. So I just choose to bask in His glory! Truly, I was witnessing the King of Glory and He had come in to speak to me as a man does to a friend!

When I saw the Lord Jesus step down into the service and walk over and speak to me face-to-face, I was changed. In a moment and in the twinkle of an eye I was transformed into one new man. When Jesus touched my hand, something happened. When Jesus gazed into my eyes, my life and nature was changed. I began to see in a new way. I began to hear in a new way. I began to think in a new way. I began to speak in a new way. I was a new creature! For about nine months after that, almost everywhere I went I saw angels and demons all the time. However, I didn't know what I was experiencing.

Today I know I was experiencing the gift of the seer anointing or the gift of discerning of spirits was activated in my life. At that time I was unchurched; I didn't know what it was; I had no theology for it. But I knew it was the Lord's will that I was seeing and hearing all these things and it was wonderful; I embraced it. The Lord began to use me in the healing ministry. I began to see all sorts of miracles, signs, and wonders—gold dust, angel feathers, tumors dissolve off of people, lots of healings, and deaf ears opening and so forth.

God used the time I was in Newfoundland to open up my spirit and my spiritual eyes to a "new dimension." The Lord began the process of teaching me to see in a new way. I was beginning to understand that I could also hear in a new way (Luke 8:18). In other words the trip to Newfoundland prophetically represented a "new found land" for me in the realm of the spirit. I am sure that it was the grace of God that allowed me to begin to operate in the seer anointing. However, I would later discover that when I appealed to the Lord to "open my eyes" and other senses to perceive elements from the spiritual dimensions and the activity of realms of heaven, He is more than willing to do so. He will do the same for you too. You can learn to see in a new way. You can learn to hear in a new way. Perhaps it is as simple as just asking? Let's do that now.

Prayer to See and Hear in a New Way

Father, Your word says that the testimony of Jesus is the spirit of prophecy. So, Lord, according to the last testimony, I ask You now to begin to help me to see in a new way. Lord, in the name of Jesus Christ, I ask You, Father, that I would begin to hear in a new way. Holy Spirit, I ask for You to guide and to teach me today. Holy Ghost, help me to learn to see and to hear in a new way. Lord, help to reveal to my spirit what Jesus desired for me to understand when He taught in Luke 8:18: "Take heed how you hear. For whoever has, to him more will be given." Lord, I am asking that more will be given to me to hear the way that You wish for me to hear, O God. And right now I thank You, Lord, for opening up my spiritual ears to hear and opening up my spiritual eyes to see in new and amazing ways. In Jesus' name I pray. Amen!

CHAPTER 10

Fiery Seraphim

After I experienced this life changing visitation of Jesus on November 25th, the Spirit of the Lord led me to the cities of St. John's and Botwood in Newfoundland. Both of these excursions proved to be a time of being stretched and prepared by the Lord for greater things.

When I arrived at St. John's, I attended two meetings held in a local church there. The Lord's Spirit was resting heavily upon me during this season. You should understand that the Spirit and glory of the Lord can rest upon you heavily at times. Yet, at other times it is like the Lord is playing hide and seek with you. The Spirit of the Lord was leading my steps in this season, and it seemed that the Lord was very close to me.

I remembered the way the Spirit had led me to travel to St. John's, so my spirit was pregnant with expectation. And I continued to pursue the Lord with all of my heart. During the meeting one night, I had an amazing encounter with the Kingdom of Heaven. I was once more under the anointing of the Holy Spirit, and I was seemingly glued to the floor. The glory and presence of the Lord was resting upon me mightily. My spiritual ears seemed to open to a much greater degree.

Here is a point of reference for you budding seers. Once you have experienced a new level of the anointing of the seer realms, you can keep it. When the Spirit of the Lord allows you to experience hearing in a new way or seeing in a new way, you can always step back into that same anointing. This is a key that can help you to massage your spiritual gifting to see and to hear from the Kingdom of Heaven. Don't get frustrated in seasons when it seems that the Spirit of the Lord is hiding from you. Just seek Him all the more and be diligent to make place for the Lord to speak to you and to show you things from His Kingdom. Remember, learning to grow and mature your seer gifting is, at times, a learning curve. Let me encourage you to persevere. You can begin to hear in a new way like the next part of this testimony illustrates.

The Tongs from the Altar

Suddenly I heard a very loud and unusual sound. I could also smell smoke and sensed that a very hot furnace was being stoked nearby. "That's weird," I thought. It seemed to me that a huge insect was buzzing around my head. However, since I was unable to move my body I could not turn my head to see what it was. The sound became louder and the buzzing was now very close to me, and I discerned the burning smell was closer to my head now. At that instant my spiritual eyes were opened and saw a large angelic creature that appeared to be a flame of fire!

Later I learned that this angel may have been seraphim like the prophet Isaiah described in Isaiah 6:6. This angelic being moved too quickly for me to focus my vision upon it to determine its exact form and appearance. One thing was certain; it smelled like smoke and had a fiery appearance! Suddenly the seraphim stopped directly over my face for an instant and I saw what looked like a glowing ember of fire being lowered onto my lips. Then the coal actually touched my lips and my mouth was instantly on fire. In fact, my whole spirit, soul, and body seemed to be ignited and to burn. This sensation lasted for days!

Often the Lord will activate your seer gifting in increments. First you hear in a new way, and then you may begin to have your discernment greatly increase to have supernatural knowledge. Then you will often begin to see in a new way and be able to visually discern the Kingdom of Heaven that is already active around you. It is a process, and occasionally it takes time.

Later that night the Spirit of the Lord spoke to me telling me to read Revelation 4 out loud. I read the scriptures over and over again: *"After these things I looked, and behold, a door standing open in heaven. And the first voice which I heard was like a trumpet speaking with me, saying, 'Come up here, and I will show you things which must take place after this.' Immediately I was in the Spirit; and behold, a throne set in heaven, and One sat on the throne"* (vv. 1-2).

This passage of scripture illustrates these Kingdom dynamics. First the Apostle John looked and he saw. Then when his seer gift was operating, he heard in a new way. And then he was launched and released into the heavenly dimensions to interact with the Kingdom of Heaven. The Lord may well use similar Kingdom dynamics to activate your seer gifting. Now let's get back to the testimony of the large angelic creature.

The Baptism of the Holy Spirit and of Fire

After a few minutes of reading this passage, the same anointing and glory that I had experienced on the night of November 25th exploded into my space again. At the same instant I heard an earsplitting whistling sound coming in my direction from the heavenly realms. I looked up to see a ball of fire descending from heaven! This supernatural fireball was plummeting from heaven right at me. It was accelerating at the speed of light! Before I could even brace myself or move out of the way, this heavenly fire slammed into my belly and I began to pray in tongues. I had no power to stop the river of heavenly language that was flowing from the very depth of my being (John 7:18).

My tattered old King James Bible was launched into the air as the ball of fire made contact with my belly. It landed on the floor with a thud. Perhaps this was the baptism of the Holy Spirit and fire? The fire seemed to be absorbed into my whole being—spirit, soul, and body. (See Matthew 3:11; Luke 3:16.) In an instant my body was on fire, and I found myself hurtling through space. I looked down and saw my body vibrating and gyrating upon the bed. My spirit was instantly lifted out of my body and could hear myself praying in tongues. In an instant my spirit was sucked through the roof of the house.

I was launched out past the atmosphere of the earth. I could see the island of Newfoundland in the distance growing smaller below me. In the darkness of the night I could see the lights of the cities and the villages of Newfoundland receding far below me. As I looked to my left, I saw that there was an angel who had taken me by my left hand and was carrying me into the spirit. I was not fearful but only astonished. The angel did not speak to me but looked at me reassuringly. As we ascended higher, I saw the sun as it began to rise in the eastern sky over Europe. After a little while, the angel set me gently down in an expansive place. The Lord was once more there.

The Sea of Glass Like Crystal

There were also four other angels present, and they seemed to be waiting for me. This heavenly place was full of light, and the floor seemed to be made of a golden substance. Worship filled the atmosphere around Christ. Jesus came directly to me and took me by the hand. The Lord then began to talk to me telling about His calling upon my life. He spoke about my inherent spiritual DNA. The Lord began to speak to me about many things. These were mostly personal things that pertained to my healing and sanctification. After a time we had walked to a place that I assumed was the shore of a crystal clear sea. Jesus revealed events to me about my life that were yet to come. In fact, we visited many places in the heavenly realms. When we went back to the place where the first angel had "dropped me off," there were four angels waiting there. These angelic beings seemed to be waiting for Christ's return.

Then Jesus spoke to me to me about these angels, telling me that He was releasing the second angel to help me minister. This angel is commissioned to help with releasing miracles and healings. You could rightly define this angelic being an angel of healing and miracles. Later the Lord said goodbye to me. I had now thought of other things I would have liked to have asked Jesus, but my time had come to an end. I was being launched back through time and space by the first strong angel. I saw the Earth below becoming larger. I saw Newfoundland and then the house I was staying in. Suddenly my spirit man passed through the roof and was sucked back into my body. I was totally covered in sweat. I had been in the spirit for about six hours. When I tried to pray a prayer of thanksgiving all that came out was a new heavenly language! I luxuriated in the glory of the Lord that was hovering in the room for several more hours and pondered the experiences in my heart.

My paradigms were being shattered and my ability to hear the Lord communicate with me was being supernaturally transformed. I was learning to trust God completely. I felt that I was supposed to travel the village of Botwood and attend more revival meetings. I was broke, in more ways than one. But I somehow had faith for the Lord to make a way where there seemed to be none. A winter storm hit the region blanketing the roads with a heavy layer of snow. Driving was slow and treacherous. I wondered if I had missed the Lord. After all, it was likely that people had died from being stranded on roads like the one we were trying to drive on in the winter here in Newfoundland.

By the grace of God, I arrived in Botwood just in time for the next revival service. A woman named Margaret approached me and my friend saying, "The Holy Spirit told me to give you a place to stay." I was extremely grateful as I had no money and no place to sleep. I was not looking forward to spending the night in a car covered by a foot of snow; and besides that, it was truly freezing outside! I graciously accepted her offer.

Prophecy!

Margaret gave me a separate room to stay in for the night. The Spirit was still resting upon me heavily. So when I closed the door, the Lord began to speak to me and the glory of God fell into the little bedroom. I started to weep at the goodness of God, and I immediately began to praise and worship the Lord. Later the Spirit led me to read from Revelation 4 again. Around 3:30 a.m. I dozed into a peaceful semi-sleep praying in the Spirit.

"Kevin get up, it is time to go to work." I opened my eyes and looked around the room. "Was that an audible voice" I wondered? I was pondering this as I looked at the clock. It was just turning 5:00 a.m. I had only been sleeping for about an hour. I sleepily said "Lord, what could you possible want me to do at this hour?" He responded, "Walk downstairs and prophesy to Margaret." I protested, "Lord I don't even know Margaret." He said, "Don't worry; I know her. Just say what I tell you to say." "But, Lord," I replied, "it is only 5:00 a.m.; and *nobody* is awake at 5:00 a.m." He answered, "Margaret is awake. She is in the kitchen. She is praying and having tea and a scone. Go to her now." This all sounded insane to me! Me? Prophesy? And what on God's green earth is a scone?

Suddenly the glory of the Lord intensified and I found myself dressed, although I do not remember actually putting on my clothing! The next thing I knew I was walking down the hallway to the downstairs. All at once there was a still small voice that began to speak into my left ear. I was hearing the secrets of Margaret's heart and detailed things about her life and current circumstances. When I walked into the kitchen, she was having tea and a scone. I asked her what she was doing, and she told me that she was praying.

She got a perplexed look on her face when I began to speak to her about angels. I was able to prophesy to her in great detail about angels. "Your angel is very precious to you, and it has a name. Your angel's name is Charity. Your very nature is much like your angel. You are full of the love of God. The Lord is going to open your eyes to see your angel again. It is going to happen soon." Somewhere in the middle of this heavenly utterance, Margaret burst into tears!

Then I noticed that gold dust was raining down on us! Gold was covering the kitchen table and our faces. After a few minutes Margret began to share with me about her life. She described to me how God had always ministered to her using the realm of angels. She offered me some tea and scones and we fellowshipped in the glory for a while. Here is a side note: scones topped with gold dust make for a hearty breakfast meal and they seem to give you a supernatural lift. In fact, after this incident I was led by the Holy Spirit into an amazing supernatural encounter on a small island called Killick Island. Even though it was actually forty degrees below zero Fahrenheit outside, I felt warm and invigorated as I walked through the town of Botwood that morning!

That incident is outlined in great detail in the book *Dancing with Angels 1* and served to give me a supernatural direction and call for the next season of my life. It was on Killick Island that the Lord commissioned me to travel to Africa. This was possibly my greatest fear! It was daunting traveling to Canada in the middle of an arctic winter. But Africa? There was no way that I could wrap my mind around that idea. I had no intention of traveling halfway around the Earth to the deep darkness of Africa! But, in the end, with God all things are possible!

Margret also gave me a copy of Benny Hinn's book *Good Morning Holy Spirit*. Later the Spirit of God prompted me to pray for three people and they were all healed. The prophecy, and now the healings were boggling my mind! I had never dreamed that God could use me to minister in miracles and healings like this. It was shortly after these experiences that the Lord directed me to extend my stay in Newfoundland. In fact, I was instructed to embark on a supernatural quest in the province. Come along on that mystical journey next!

CHAPTER 11

Daisy's Cabin up in the Wilderness

It was during this time as these supernatural experiences were unfolding that the Lord spoke to me very clearly. The Lord told me that He wanted me to go up into a cabin in the wilderness of Newfoundland. I didn't have any money; I was coming out of this place of addiction and drugs and all these terrible things. So, I could not imagine how God could make a way for this to happen. After all, I needed to get back to America and work, right? I didn't even know how I was going to pay for lunch that day.

So when God spoke to me and said, "I want you to go up into the mountains in Newfoundland, and I am going to meet you there," in my flesh I thought, "Oh, that'll never happen." But in my spirit I said, "Oh! OK, Lord. Sure!" This is a key that can surely help you to activate the seer anointing in your life. You must be obedient when the Lord asks you do something even if you see no possible way or the prophetic act makes no sense in the natural realm. *Remember, your spirit knows a lot more than your carnal mind does about the Kingdom of Heaven.*

So a few days later on Sunday, December 9, 2001, I was back where it all started in Living Waters Ministries, in Springdale, Newfoundland, Canada. I had invested the last few days resting in the Lord and seeking His face. I was looking to Him for direction and wisdom. When the worship service started, I was no closer to having any real direction. However, in my heart I just purposed to praise the Lord. So I'm in the church and worship is going on and I'm dancing around praising God. I was giving Him praise because I had experienced this face-to-face encounter with Jesus. I'm thinking about what I'm going to do. Jesus had called me to the nations. He said, *"Go into all the world teaching them to observe all things that I have commanded you; and lo, I am with you always, even to the end of the age."*

But I'm like, "Me?" and thinking about how this is going to happen. I was struggling inside. I had rent due in America, and I was not working. On top of that I had exhausted all of my funds traveling to these revival meetings where I sowed all of my earthy loonies and toonies into the offering plate. (By the way, loonies and toonies are one- and two-dollar Canadian coins). Just about then this little lady, an elder in the church named Daisy, comes up to me and stops me. Daisy says, "Kevin, God spoke to me in prayer this morning about you." And I said, "Oh, that's nice!" I was just about to dismiss her and continue to twirl around the altar. You never know who God's going to use to speak the word of the Lord into your life.

Ascending to the Hill of the Lord

But somehow I knew it was the Lord speaking to me. So I stopped rotating and looked into her beautiful shining eyes. Her eyes radiated a lot like Jesus' eyes at that moment. I said, "Daisy, that's nice. What did He say?" She said, "The Lord said I'm supposed to let you take time to be alone with Him in my cabin up in the wilderness. The cabin is up in the mountains." I almost passed out, but I felt like I was floating about a foot off of the ground! When the service was over, I began to make arrangements to travel up into the mountains to visit with the Lord. It seemed to me I remembered reading in the Bible where God had led other people to go up on mountains so He could speak to them. Maybe I was on to something? Hallelujah!

So off I went into the mountains of Newfoundland in the midst of January. It was snowing and really freezing up there. On the way a part of me was longing for the crystal clear waters of Cinnamon Bay, St. John in the United States Virgin Islands, but those thoughts soon passed. I was on the way up to the cabin. My spirit was full of expectation, and my soul was full of trepidation. Perhaps I should be returning to America and seeking to find some work to pay my overdue bills. What was my landlord saying? Then I remembered! The Holy Spirit had instructed me to pay the rent through January before I left! Thanks, Holy Ghost! That memory took some pressure off!

My new friend Margaret had given me the book *Good Morning Holy Spirit*. As I was traveling ever higher on the mountain, that made me smile. I was really excited to be going up on the mountain to meet with the Lord. One reason was because I assumed that I was supposed to read Benny Hinn's book in the cabin. I was really looking forward to reading the book. So when we finally reached the cabin, I stoked the fire. It was totally freezing up there! Let me explain something to you: Newfoundland in December is cold. I mean really, really cold! Apparently the bitter arctic winters are great for cod, but not so much for me at this season.

Once it warmed up a bit, I took a mental inventory. I was going to be in Daisy's cabin for three days. I had a little canvas backpack and in it were all the earthly possessions that I had at that moment in the wilderness of Canada: the book *Good Morning Holy Spirit*, my old beat-up King James Bible, a package of crackers, three cans of soup, some bottled water, and some peanut butter and a loaf of bread. That's all I had. But then I remembered that I had the Holy Spirit who was guiding me and leading me. So I relaxed.

Then everybody left. I walked out on the porch to watch them go and stood there for a moment listening and watching. I was seeing and hearing. When the sound of the car's engine completely faded, it dawned upon me that it was incredibly silent and incredibly cold in this place by the mountain lake. I was truly all alone in the wilderness of Newfoundland. I couldn't leave if I had wanted to. There was no phone and no running water, and it was impossible for me to walk out of those mountains. It was just me and God. Well, of course there was the ever-present freezing cold; and, thank God, plenty of firewood and matches!

When I stepped back through the door, the same power and the same glory of God that was present on November 25th when Jesus stood over me invaded Daisy's little mountain cabin. I moved past the stove and settled upon the couch and the glory pinned me to the quilt there. I rested in the glory for hours unable to move. I was only able to worship Him. I wept, I laughed, and I prayed in tongues some. But at other times the power of God was too strong and I could only behold His glory. The glory continued to minister to me in this sovereign fashion for another twenty-four hours or so. From time to time the glory would lift a little. This allowed me to stoke the fire. But most of the time I was pinned to the couch by the power and glory of the King!

I no longer cared about working. I no longer cared about returning to America. I no longer cared about snorkeling. I no longer cared about overdue rent. All I wanted was to be with Him. I just wanted to rest in His glory. I just wanted to lay there and let the memories of the fantastic supernatural encounters of the last few days percolate up into my spirit time and time again. I just wanted to remember what the beautiful eyes of Jesus looked like. I just wanted to feel His unfathomable love again. I just wanted to be in His presence. What a glorious heavenly time we had at Daisy's little mountain cabin, the Spirit of the Lord and me!

An Angel of Revelation

After about thirty hours or so, I felt a release and prepared a can of Campbell's Chicken Noodle Soup and two peanut butter sandwiches and had a warm filling dinner. Then after eating heartily, I had stoked the fire for the evening. The sun was just beginning to set behind the fir trees near the lake. The lake was covered with ice and a fresh blanket of snow, but it seemed to be glowing with a beautiful red sheen at that instant. It was breathtaking. It was stunningly beautiful as the sun was setting, and it was also stunningly cold. A thought trickled into my mind: "Lord, perhaps we *could* go snorkeling someday where it is a little warmer?"

After my dinner I thought, "OK, time to read *Good Morning Holy Spirit*." So I went over to my little backpack and reached in. I was going to grab *Good Morning Holy Spirit*. But the Lord stopped me and said, "No, Kevin, not that book. I want you to read the Book of Acts." So I grabbed my old King James Bible instead and took it to the table. And as I placed that old King James Bible on the wooden table, the sun was just about to set and the Bible seemed to supernaturally pop open to the very first title page of the Book of Acts.

For an instant I glanced up to see that an angel of revelation was standing there silhouetted against the picture window with the bright red Newfoundland sunset blazing behind him. I saw him as he quickly moved his hands away from the Bible and he shot me a furtive smile. It occurred to me that I had seen this angel before. Of course, this was one of the four angels that Jesus had introduced me to in the heavenly realms. In an instant the angel vanished in plain sight! And the glory of God fell on that place and upon me again. For the next two days the Lord, the Holy Spirit, took me scripture by scripture through the whole Book of Acts.

Our Amazing God

It was amazing! I would ask the Holy Spirit about the meaning of a certain scripture, and He would speak to me about it. In

Daisy's Cabin up in the Wilderness

fact, the voice of the Holy Ghost may have been audible, as it was so powerful and clear to me there in Daisy's little cabin. The Spirit of God was teaching me to hear in a new way. It was during this season that I became much more inclined to hear the Holy Spirit speaking to me and learned to recognize the voice of the Holy Ghost. It is imperative that we hear the voice of God well at this hour. Hearing God is another aspect of the seer anointing, and you must allow the Spirit of God to train you in this regard.

The Lord was teaching me to see and to hear in new ways. My life was transformed and the Lord birthed the ministry that He has called my wife Kathy and me to be stewards over in Newfoundland. Perhaps one day I will return? I learned something as the person of the Holy Spirit took me through the entire Book of Acts, scripture by scripture. It is not over. The Spirit of God is still writing it. In fact, the Lord is seeking to use you to write the final installments of the Acts of the Apostles. The Lord wants to use you in the same ministry of power and signs and wonders that were released in the early church. What is the key to unlocking your inherent God-ordained DNA to step into these amazing aspects of Christ's Kingdom? In my opinion, it is learning to see in a new way and learning to hear in a new way.

Later when I was released by the Holy Spirit to read Benny Hinn's book *Good Morning Holy Spirit*, I was astonished to discover that Pastor Benny has experienced an encounter with the person of the Holy Spirit almost exactly like the encounter that I had just walked through! God in His infinite wisdom sent the confirmation for the experience that He already knew that

I would walk through with me into the mountains of Newfoundland. What an amazing God! Oh, how I praise Him for this even now! "O Lord, even if I had ten thousand tongues I could never praise You enough for the amazing transformation that You orchestrated in my life!"

The key is Jesus. We need to learn to become transformed into the very image of the Lord and then we can see and hear like Christ. We can do those things that we see our Father doing, and we can say those things that we hear our Father saying.

"Eye has not seen, nor ear heard, Nor have entered into the heart of man The things which God has prepared for those who love Him" (1 Corinthians 2:9). God wants to do those same things in your life. What I'm talking about are the dynamics of the seer anointing. The Lord truly wants us to learn to see and to hear in a new way. After this encounter in Daises cabin God began to do a supernatural acceleration in my life and He opened up the doors for me to travel to the nations, as He had told me to do. In the next chapter we will look at several keys that can help you to activate your seer gifting in fullness.

CHAPTER 12

What Is Normal Christianity?

From the time that I returned to America from Canada in 2001, I was, as you can imagine, totally ruined for "normal" Christianity. I came from a season of incredible visitations, experiencing the glory realms every day and constant angelic encounters to step back into life and church as "normal"! Attending a worship service once a week was not satisfying my hunger for more of Him! However, because I had never been taught nor had I ever seen another model to commune with God, I continued to attend church. In fact, I attended church a lot and from there I continued to encounter a great deal of resistance to the ministry that the Lord had called me to. I was still expected to clean toilets and to change light bulbs for the most part.

Now, hear my heart; there is absolutely nothing wrong with service and working for the church. However, at times that is not the same thing as serving and seeking to expand the Kingdom of Heaven. I write more about this dynamic in the book *Unlocking the Hidden Mysteries of the Powers of the Age to Come* if you are interested in reading my ideas along this line.

However, I briefly want to touch on this misnomer that is in operation in many places.

I believe that the church should empower and equip the people of God. Learn to serve Him and His Kingdom and seek to be empowered and equipped to expand the Kingdom of God (not so much the ministry or church). Seek to be activated to demonstrate the Kingdom of Heaven, not in word alone but in power. You could say that this is an apostolic mindset. You should expect to see miracles, signs, and wonders in your life every day. If not, then perhaps you should question why signs and wonders are not happening in your sphere of influence.

Perhaps one reason may be because you are not seeing and hearing the way that Jesus encourages you that you can. Perhaps your discernment is dull, as is written about in the book of the prophet Isaiah 6: 9-10: *"Go, and tell this people: 'Keep on hearing, but do not understand; Keep on seeing, but do not perceive.' Make the heart of this people dull, And their ears heavy, And shut their eyes; Lest they see with their eyes, And hear with their ears, And understand with their heart, And return and be healed."*

I hope and pray that the Spirit of God will use this book to help activate the gifting and anointing to see and hear (the seer anointing) in your life and in your sphere of influence. I pray that your life would be transformed and changed. I pray that you would receive total healing for your eyes and ears. I pray that the testimonies that the Holy Spirit outlined for me to place in this book would be prophetic promises for you according to the principle of Revelation 19:10: *"The testimony of Jesus is the spirit of prophesy."* Having said all of that, for my entire life I had been taught or thought that the only place I could find God was in the church. Today I have been given the understanding that I can have a close and personal relationship and communion with the Creator of heaven and earth outside the four walls of a church building.

As Mixed Up as a Bumble Bee in a Tornado

So I attended churches about five to seven times a week after these experiences. I was hearing a lot of different doctrine but I was not growing or maturing a lot from the teaching I was getting. I am fortunate that I did not become as mixed up as a bumble bee in a tornado! You need to guard your heart regarding what you see and hear and allow into your spirit. Your spirit is like a well. Keep it clean; don't pollute your spirit. This is another key to developing your seer gift. Guard your heart with all diligence. We see this important principle outlined in Proverbs 4:23: *"Keep your heart with all diligence, For out of it spring the issues of life."*

One Sunday the pastor would welcome me, smile at me, and shake my hand. The next day he would tell other pastors that I had demons and a rebellious spirit. Why did he say these things? One reason was because I was out in the streets praying for the sick and seeing the lost saved. I was going into the local hospital and healing the sick and leading patients to Jesus as Savior at times. In his opinion I should have been changing lights and painting the hallway of the church.

Now, let me say this: I did those things. In fact, I cleaned the bathrooms of one church every week for over a year. I vacuumed the carpets; I straightened up the kitchen and washed the dishes. Those things are great. Serving the church or a ministry is a wonderful thing to do. There is true impartation that comes from serving an anointed ministry or church. If you caught that I was inferring that there are un-anointed ministries or churches; uh, you get the idea.

Suddenlies

However, if you are a ministry leader I want to speak to you directly now. Look for suddenlies. The Lord is saving the most vile and repulsive people by the power of His Spirit, such people like myself. He is empowering them to win the great last days harvest, and many will not fit the mold that you are expecting. They may come with tattoos; they may come with terrible reputations and really bad breath. They will come from the depths of addiction and abuse.

Expect God to start sending them to you. I think of my friend who is the lead guitarist for Korn. Wow, what an amazing testimony! Brian "Head" Welch is now a hard-core, born-again, on fire evangelist who is traveling all over the earth as a witness for Jesus! Praise the Lord! You better get ready for suddenlies. And, oh, by the way, many will come fully activated and experiencing the seer realms, though they may not have revelation or understanding of the gift they are walking in! You may be called to disciple them and not quench the fire of the Spirit that rests upon them!

That was the position that I found myself in December 2001 and later in 2002. I was on fire! In fact, one pastor actually sent a local evangelist to me privately and told me that I needed to "tone it down" and that I was too zealous for the Lord! In the midst of all of this, I pressed into the Kingdom until I ripped and rended the heavens open over my life back in the USA.

I was starting to discern angelic activity and was encountering the glory realms consistently. After a while I started to ascend to the hill of the Lord nearly every day. Let me state that a little more clearly. Jesus was inviting me to travel into heaven all the time! I would go up into heaven and fellowship with Jesus. I would see and hear what Jesus was showing me, and miracles and great favor began to happen in my life every day. The Lord told me to write down the experiences I was walking through in heaven in 2002. A decade later in 2012 those depictions of the places in heaven became the book *Angels in the Realms of Heaven*.

Killick Island

While I was on Killick Island in the bay of Botwood, Newfoundland, Canada, the Lord had birthed a passion for winning souls in my heart. That occurred in November 2001. The Lord had spoken to me in an audible voice on Killick Island, instructing me to travel to Africa for evangelism and training. I had told the local pastor of my desire to go to Africa; and, as you can imagine, I was not really encouraged by his words. However, I knew that the Lord was in this African excursion. Somehow, I was certain that Africa was for me at this season. Although, the thought of traveling to Africa was one of my worst fears and nightmares!

Through a series of supernatural miracles of provision and angelic intervention, I traveled to Tanzanian, in East Africa, in 2002. Today King of Glory Ministries International is still ministering the love of the Father to widows and orphans in that nation (and other nations) 365 days of the year. Eventually, by the grace of God, I was able to lead tens of thousands to Christ as Savior in Africa. Can you say suddenly?

On Tuesday, May 28, 2002, I found myself in the Tilapia Hotel in Mwanza, Tanzania. After I had been interceding and praying in tongues for about three hours, I saw the heavens rip open. Jesus descended a second time into the terrestrial realm to visit me just as He had done in Canada on November 25, 2001. The Lord stood over me for about three and one-half to four hours speaking to me and teaching me. The whole time He was standing over me, I witnessed perhaps hundreds of angels which were ascending and descending upon Jesus (John 5:19). He would point and send them out to different areas of Africa. (I write about this testimony in the book *Dancing with Angels 1*, if you would like to read that testimony in more detail.)

As I lay there listening to Jesus and talking to Him, I was unable to move. Once more I found myself glued to the cold tile floor of the bungalow. I was no longer in a hotel room in Tanzania. Rather, I had been translated to what appeared to be the sea of glass like crystal in the heavenly realms (Revelation 4:6). Perhaps it would be more accurate to say that the heavenly realms invaded my space here on earth. During this whole visitation Jesus was assigning these angels to many different nations. In between the times that the Lord was instructing and sending these mighty angels, He was speaking to me about the seer anointing.

The Seers of Old

Jesus said, "Kevin, I want you to study about the seers of old." I said, "Well, I don't know what a seer is, Lord." Remember that this was back in 2002 and I was a fairly new believer in this Man named Christ. He told me to start my reading in 1 Samuel, chapter 9. *"Formerly in Israel, when a man went to inquire of God, he spoke thus: 'Come, let us go to the seer'; for he who is now called a prophet was formerly called a seer"* (v. 9). And He began to teach me and speak to me about the seer anointing for about three hours. I didn't know anything about seers back then. And to be quite honest, I don't have the full revelation about the seer realms now. But I have some understanding, and I believe God wants me to share what He has given me with you. Specifically, the Lord instructed me to share the testimonies and prayers that are in this book with you, the reader. On February 25, 2014, I experienced another angelic visitation in my prayer room in Moravian Falls, North Carolina, and the Lord released some additional revelation concerning the seer anointing to me from Psalm 24. That revelation is the crux of this book.

So going back to February 25, 2001, the Lord called me to teach the things that He has commanded. In May of 2002 the Lord instructed me to begin to study the "seers of old." I have been faithful and have pressed into studying the seers of old in the scripture for twelve years as of this writing. Later in 2007 the Lord gave me more revelation concerning the seer anointing and His seers during a visitation to heaven. And then there was the encounter that transpired on February 25, 2014. All of these events are woven together in a tapestry of grace and revelation. By the grace of God, allow me to unpack the rest of the testimony now!

The Season of the Golden Eagle

Later, God gave me my beautiful wife, Kathy, and accelerated the ministry even more. We had a home on 11200 Kensington Avenue, in Kansas City, Missouri. During this time a large golden eagle had begun to visit our home. It would come to the backyard and eat fish out of the lake there. The Lord had spoken to me about the golden eagle and its relationship to the seer anointing. So for three weeks I had pressed through doing research about golden eagles and the seer anointing. In the Bible when we read things about mounting up with wings like eagles (Isaiah 40:31), it's talking about the golden eagle. I believe many scriptural references to eagles refer to the golden eagle. It's my conclusion and opinion that the golden eagle represents the seer anointing.

During this season in 2007, I had been fasting for three days when Jesus appeared to me in a dream and told me to "Google the golden eagle." When I glanced at the clock it was 4:20 a.m. (Acts 4:20). I got up and surfed the Internet for revelation on the golden eagle! I saw images of the same kind of bird that was fishing in our back yard. I am not an ornithologist, but I believe the eagle I was seeing was an adolescent golden eagle. I continued to fast and pray. I started meditating on Acts 4:19-20 for the next three weeks. I read those two scriptures hundreds of times. Finally the Lord highlighted a section—*"We cannot but speak the things which we have seen and heard"*—and I had an epiphany. God wants us to speak and declare the things that we see and hear. He wants us to hear and to see in a new way!

Soon I realized that this golden eagle was indeed a sign and wonder. I have come to the conclusion that the golden eagle represents the "seer anointing" and the release of the gift of discerning of spirits. The golden eagle's appearance in Kansas City led to the revelation that the Lord was about to release the prophetic gift of the "seer" anointing into many cities around the earth. Kathy and I shared this message in many nations in 2007, encouraging people to prepare their hearts and spirits for the seer realms. As we traveled we also discovered that golden eagles were returning to many cities in America and throughout the world.

We were also given a newspaper article about a pair of golden eagles that had built a large nest in one of the largest cities in the Netherlands. Golden eagles were being restored to health and were beginning to show up in a lot of cities around the earth! Soon I began to see many media articles about this phenomenon. We believe the restoration of the eagles were signs in the natural of what the Lord is doing in the spirit. The seer anointing is also beginning to be released and restored in mass in many cities and in many nations throughout the earth as the Holy Spirit pours out the gift of discerning of spirits. This phenomenon has only accelerated since 2007.

During this season in 2007, I prayed continuously asking the Lord to give me a revelation about all these things that were happening. I was in my prayer room on April 20 (Acts 4:20) when I was caught up into heaven where I came to sit beside Jesus on a large granite bench in the heavenly realms. Once again the Lord began to speak to me about the seer anointing. I'm sitting there beside Jesus, and I see all these beautiful mountains in the distance but I can't see them very clearly. The Lord takes His right index finger and He points and says, "Kevin, look!" (By the way the right index finger represents the office of the prophet.)

When I followed where Jesus was pointing, it was like my vision multiplied and I was able to see much more clearly. This happened two or three times. Finally my vision became so clear that I could see a golden eagle's nest, even though it was miles and miles away. I saw eggs in this golden eagle's nest that were beginning to hatch. I saw these little eaglets begin to come out of the eggs and they began to chirp. They were saying, "Seers; seers; seers." I had this revelation that God is birthing and raising up seers all over the earth at this hour. These seers are being ordained and called by God in the heavenly realms. It was later that year that we began to see and learn about the restoration of the golden eagles in the natural.

I then turned to my left and looked into the eyes of the Lord, and I was catapulted back through time and space; I went from Kansas City and Heaven back to Africa in 2002. So I went backwards in time and from North America to Heaven to Africa. I relived the whole experience where Jesus stood over me for three and one-half hours and taught me about the seer anointing. I was really glad because I was able to make better notes. (Here is a key: when God begins to give you seer experiences, write your encounters down.) Now I am in Africa and I'm lying on the sea of glass like crystal again, and I hear the Lord teaching me about the seer anointing and the seers of old all over again. I relive the entire experience that happened about five years earlier. As the experience was drawing to a conclusion, I suddenly hear the screech of a golden eagle. Instantly I find myself being catapulted back through time and space to the granite bench in the heavenly places where Jesus is sitting and speaking to me about the seers of old (Ephesians 1:20).

A Paradigm Shift

I'm thinking to myself, "Wait a minute. Am I in Kansas City, am I in Heaven, or am I in Africa?" The answer is that I was probably in all three places at once. In the seer realm or the glory realms there is no time as we know it and there is no distance as we know it. And that's going to be one of the hidden mysterious things God is going to release to His people. He's going to give us the liberty to be translated from one place to another. The key is to be able to see and hear what God is doing. The key is to be able to see and hear in a new way, with a Kingdom mindset. It is a paradigm shift.

At that point in 2007, the Lord spoke to me and said, "Kevin, the day will come when I will release you to be able to teach My people about the seer anointing." You are reading this book because of that supernatural directive of the Lord. I believe that there is a grace placed upon our life for impartation of gifts—impartation to see and hear well from the Lord.

I believe that you are not reading this book by accident! I prophesy that you will receive an impartation by the Spirit of God. You are reading this book because God has called you to a specific task, at a specific time, in a specific place. A place where the heavens are going to open and God is going to release a supernatural blessing upon you and yours. We have looked at several testimonies of Jesus concerning the seer realms. Let's now move back to Psalm 24 to discover the hidden mysteries of Psalm 24 in relation to the seer anointing. This is one of the two anointings and blessings that God revealed to me during an angelic visitation on February 25, 2014, from Psalm 24. Let's discover those hidden mysteries of Psalm 24 next!

Prayer for Boldness to See and Hear in a New Way

Father, in Jesus' name I ask that You grant to Your servant boldness to see and hear the way that You want me to see and hear. It is right in Your sight, O God, to listen and to hear You more clearly rather than listen to the doctrine of man. Lord, I ask that You open up the seer realms to me so that I am empowered by Your Spirit to see and hear clearly from Your Kingdom. Then I shall decree: "For I cannot but speak the things which I have seen and heard." In Jesus' name, I pray. Amen.

CHAPTER 13

Unearthing the Hidden Mysteries of Psalm 24

I believe when David wrote this psalm, he was writing under a brilliant prophetic anointing. What he has written has such depth to it. Psalm 24 is like a beautiful diamond. If you look at the different facets of a diamond under sunlight, it can refract many different outpourings of color. It's the same with the word of God; when we get revelation from the Spirit, the word of God can take on meanings that we may not have seen before. That's why there are hidden mysteries in this destiny-centric Psalm.

Let's look at this Psalm of David in more detail. Starting in verse 1, we read, *"The earth is the LORD's and all its fullness, The world and those who dwell therein."* The word translated "Lord" in this verse is Jehovah, the God of Israel. We need to understand who King David is referring to in this entire passage. That's important—the Lord God Almighty. Remember, we are triune beings who serve a triune God—God the Father, God the Son, and God the Holy Spirit. The Trinity is a profound mystery. I believe David is specifically describing the Father and His throne in Psalm 24.

We go on with verse 2: *"For He has founded it upon the seas, And established it upon the waters."* "Founded it" means to set it in place or to create a thing. We know that in the beginning the Father spoke into the hovering of the Spirit to create all things (Genesis 1:1-9). "Established" means to prepare or create order from chaos. What we are talking about is the terrestrial realm—the realm that we live in. We breathe the air of the terrestrial realm; our bodies are part of the terrestrial realm. In my opinion, the terrestrial realm is just as supernatural as the heavenly realms; but we often don't discern, appreciate, or see that mystical nature of the earth and the earthly realms. Why, you might ask? Because the earth is the Lord's and all of the fullness thereof, and God is a supernatural Being and He created the earth in a supernatural fashion.

More of the blessings of God and the hidden mysteries contained in this supernatural Psalm begin to unfold in verse 3: *"Who may ascend into the hill of the Lord?"* It amazed me when the Lord showed this to me. I have been reading and studying Psalm 24 for more than twelve years and had never *"seen"* these spiritual truths (the gospel)! What it really means when it says to *"ascend into the hill of the Lord"* is to move into another place or dimension. *"The hill"* means the mountain or habitation of God. So, really, when it says, *"Who may ascend into the hill of the Lord?"* it's really saying, "Who may ascend into the dwelling place or habitation of God or the spiritual realm?"

Mount the Heights of Heaven

Do you want to do that? We can do that at this hour. It's not hyper-spiritual. You can go up onto the mountain of the Lord much like I went up into the mountains of Newfoundland. Just as with that supernatural testimony, it may be uncomfortable for you. You may prefer warm places and the Lord may send you to the coldest. You may prefer to be comfortable, but the Lord might choose to stretch you. You may prefer to stay in your place of comfort and security, but the Lord may send you to a place of uncertainly where you must focus and depend totally upon Him alone. But you can ascend onto the mountain of the Lord. You can ascend to His holy place. Just embrace such a spiritual journey! Even Jesus went up onto the mountain of the Lord from time to time (see Matthew 14:23; Luke 9:28; John 9:17).

How did Jesus do and see the things His Father was doing (John 5:19)? He ascended into the hill of the Lord. The Lord Jesus was able to see, discern, and hear what His Father was doing at all times. Jesus was able to see in a new way. Jesus saw and heard in a different way than most of us. Jesus was able to pass through the heavenly realms (through open heavens-spiritual gates- portals of glory) to ascend the hill of the Lord and visit with His Father. There on the hill of the Lord, Jesus garnered supernatural revelation from the heavenly realms. That is why Jesus could teach us in Luke 8:18: *"Therefore take heed how you hear. For whoever has, to him more will be given; and whoever does not have, even what he seems to have will be taken from him."*

This is really Jesus' role as a royal priest according the order of Melchizedek. I want to examine the word *ascend*. In the Strong's Hebrew Concordance it is #H5927, *alah*, which means to ascend or to go up or to actively mount the heights or the heavenly realms. A practical modern-day example would be the testimony I shared with you about being in Kansas City and being plucked up into Heaven. I ascended to the hill of the Lord to see what Jesus wanted to show me.

I will share other biblical examples with you as we move forward. The word *ascend* can have a lot of different meanings, both literally and figuratively. It can mean to rise up, to be caused to ascend up at once or immediately. It can mean to break up, to bring up, to be carried up, to be cast up, to be seen, or to be shown a mysterious or hidden treasure. Do you want that? You need to ascend into the hill of the Lord. Jehovah wants us to see in a new way so that He can show us and teach us to see with a heavenly paradigm and with transformed minds (Romans 12:1-2).

Ascend can also mean to climb up, to cause or make a way for, to come up, to be cut off from the lower parts or lesser realms. How does that sound? This is not something that has to be a hyper-spiritual experience. We can become so in tune with the Spirit of God that the seer anointing can activate in our life in such a consistent way that we walk in the heavenly realms no matter where we are. We begin to see and hear heavenly things and spiritual things all around us. Scripturally it is called the gift of discerning of spirits; I also call it the seer anointing.

These first three verses in Psalm 24 speak of two realms—the terrestrial realm and the spiritual realm. When we have the ability and the grace of God, we can ascend into the spiritual realm. We can ascend to the mountain or habitation of the Lord, which is in the spiritual realm. It is actually the very first thing we see in the Bible in Genesis 1:1: *"In the beginning God created the heavens and the earth."*

So, there is a spiritual realm which is all around us constantly. The scriptures call it the heavens (plural). I should point out that heaven is not necessarily "up"; we can *go up* into heaven but heaven can also *come down* upon us. We can perceive, see, hear, taste, smell, touch, and or discern the heavenly realms around us at all times. This is truly seeing in a new way. You can *learn to see* with your tongue, your nose, your ears, and your hands.

The word *ascend* can also mean to be exalted, to excel, to fetch up, or to be fetched up or caught up. So another biblical example of ascending to the hill of the Lord that is commonly used to teach these things would be in the writings of Apostle Paul in 2 Corinthians 12:2: *"I know a man in Christ who fourteen years ago—whether in the body I do not know, or whether out of the body I do not know* [whether in the terrestrial or the spiritual realm], *God knows—such a one was* caught up *to the third heaven."* "Caught up" here means to be plucked or taken away by force.

See into the Heavenly Dimensions

Would you like God to just pluck you or take you away by force in to the heavenly realms like He did with me, taking me up to the granite bench in heaven? I believe that He can do that for you. One reason why I believe that is because over these past twelve years I have taught about these things and I have prayed for people to receive impartation. As a result we have received many testimonies from people who see Jesus, who visit Heaven, who have their spiritual eyes opened to see into the heavenly dimensions.

Do you want to have your spiritual eyes opened to see into the other dimensions that the Lord God created in the beginning? Would you like to see God's angelic beings? If so, seeing God's angels is a good thing; but spiritual vision is actually elementary in the Kingdom of Heaven. If God opens up your spiritual eyes to see angels that means He has a purpose for it—to help you recreate Christ in your sphere of influence.

As we continue studying the word *ascend*, we find that in 2 Corinthians 12:2 it means to be made to go up and or away, to increase, to be increased, to be lifted up, to become light, or to be recreated. That's what we really need. We need to be recreated into the very image of Jesus, and then we need to begin to do those things that we see and hear our Father doing. This is not hyper-spiritual doctrine; it's the Bible. *Ascend* also means to mount up, to be offered up, to be perfected, or to put on perfection. It means to be preferred by God (Jehovah), or to put on Christlike character. All of these descriptions illustrate seeing in a heavenly or new way.

This word *ascend* can also mean to be raised, recovered, restored, to be made to rise up, or to move upward or in a heavenly direction or into a heavenly dimension. Do you know there are heavenly dimensions all around us? God can take us up and can give us supernatural revelation about our callings or our earthly mission in His Kingdom. This can happen any time and at any place if we are willing and sensitive to the Spirit to see and to hear from heaven. The testimony I shared about being launched into heaven after I was baptized in the Holy Spirit with fire in St. John's Newfoundland in November 2001 is a good example of this dynamic.

Do you realize that God has a preordained destiny for you? God has something He has ordained for you to do. He knit your destiny into the DNA of your cells when you were woven together in your mother's womb by the Spirit of God (Psalm 139:13, NIV). You were created by God for His purposes. When we begin to have the seer anointing activated in our lives, we begin to see and hear what God's destiny and purposes for our lives are. We obtain a supernatural purpose and the grace of God to accomplish it. Our minds are transformed, our paradigms shift, and we begin to see and hear in an extraordinarily supernatural way.

Moving Out from Beersheba

Another biblical example of this type of ascending or supernatural grace and favor would be in the life of Jacob. We find Jacob's story in Genesis 28:10-13:

> *Now Jacob went out from Beersheba and went toward Haran. So he came to a certain place [Bethel] and stayed there all night, because the sun had set. And he took one of the stones of that place and put it at his head, and he lay down in that place to sleep. Then he dreamed, and behold, a ladder was set up on the earth, and its top reached to heaven; and there the angels of God were*

> ***ascending*** *[same Hebrew word] and descending on it. And behold, the* Lord *stood above it and said: "I am the* Lord *[Jehovah] God of Abraham your father and the God of Isaac; the land on which you lie I will give to you and your descendants" (emphasis added).*

The important point to see about this scripture is the word *ascending* in verse 12. The ladder that the angels were ascending upon was going through a portal, a spiritual gate, into the heavenly realms. Jacob came to a certain place where this ascending and descending was happening. It's the same word as in Psalm 24:3: *"Who may **ascend** into the hill of the* Lord*"* (emphasis added). So clearly, when we look at this, what we see is an open Heaven encounter with Jehovah. We see a place where there was a spiritual gate open and a man witnessed activity in the spirit realm.

Another way to say it would be that Jacob had the seer anointing activated in his life and he saw and heard in the spiritual realm; he saw the heavenly realms ascending and descending. Jacob received a supernatural blessing from this visitation. This is very similar to my testimony I shared with you about November 25, 2001, when I saw the angels of the Lord descend into the little church in Springdale, Newfoundland, Canada, soon to be followed by Jesus. I saw Him descend and ascend. God is still doing this today. It can still happen. I want to encourage you that you can have supernatural heavenly visitations like Jacob experienced in your life today. Some of us need to move out of Beersheba (from the known or place of oaths or place of promises) and into Bethel (the place of fulfilled oaths and visitations).

The next thing we see in Genesis 28 is in verse 13, where *"the LORD stood above it and said: 'I am the LORD* [Jehovah] *God of Abraham your father and the God of Isaac'"* and He releases and decrees heavenly blessings and the favor of God over Jacob and his progeny. How would you like to have an increase in the favor of God that rests upon your life? This is the same God, the same Jehovah, who we see in Psalm 24. We need to move from living a lifestyle of waiting upon prophetic promises to come true and move into a place where we see the manifestation of the Kingdom of Heaven in our lives. Learning to see or discern spiritual gates and being geographically obedient to position ourselves under or in open heavens will help us to move into Bethel or into the manifestation of the blessings of God.

What I want you to see is that there is a God-ordained blessing released by Jehovah in circumstances like this. When you come to a place (both geographically and spiritually) where the heavens open up over your life, ascending and descending occurs; the seer anointing manifests. The Kingdom of Heaven comes down and the angels of the Lord are free to ascend and descend to minister *to* you and also *for* you! The Kingdom comes (manifests).

The Lord releases His angels to go forth and perform the words of the decrees and heavenly blessings that God speaks over your life and over your progeny. Jehovah wants to release supernatural blessing and favor over and upon your life in a lavish way. Everything that you place your hands to will just seem to prosper! Psalm 24 has hidden keys that can accelerate this process in your life. Let's begin to search for those keys now! In the next chapter we will start to learn how to cooper-<u>ate with God to release this same types of heavenly blessings and supernatural favor into our lives.</u>

Prayer for Manifestations of the Kingdom

Lord, I thank You that Your Kingdom is a supernatural place. Today I choose to recognize that You created the heavenly and the earth. The earth is Yours, Lord, and it is a supernatural place. Today, Lord, I ask You in the mighty Name of Jesus to help me to discern and perceive the supernatural aspects of the terrestrial or earthly realms. Give me eyes to see and discern the places and times where You open the heavens over my life. In Jesus' name I pray. Amen.

CHAPTER 14

Discovering the Keys of Psalm 24

Jesus said that He would give us the keys to the Kingdom of Heaven (Matthew 16:19). In Psalm 24, verses 3 and 4, we see four of those supernatural keys that can help us to access this realm of the Kingdom of God. *"Who may **ascend** into the hill of the LORD? Or who may stand in His holy place?"* (emphasis added). In verse 4 it tells us who: *"He who has clean hands and a pure heart, Who has not lifted up his soul to an idol, Nor sworn deceitfully."* This passage is a Hebraism. What it is speaking about is living a life of integrity before both God and man. If you want to have the seer anointing activated in your life, you must live a lifestyle of integrity before God and man; you must walk in holiness. There is no other way. This is nonnegotiable.

The first key is to have clean hands, which means to be undefiled by the world's standards with our ethics and our mindset. "Clean hands" is also a reference to a person's works and actions—the works of your hands. This speaks of honesty and integrity with your actions in daily activities; it speaks of living a lifestyle of holiness. That is a key that we cannot overlook.

The second key we see in this passage of scripture is a pure heart. A pure heart is an undefiled heart, a clean heart, or a heart that does not conceal evil things or treacherous concepts. We deal honestly and we walk in light with our brothers and sisters in the Body of Christ and also those in the world. We live honorably before both God and man.

A third key in verse 4 is not lifting up our hearts to an idol. Many people dismiss the notion that they may harbor idols today. But we must realize that some of us do engage in idolatry and do have idols in our hearts. Perhaps we are unaware of this, but it is nonetheless still a great offence to the Sprit of God. This is one thing I have discovered that will keep people from stepping into the seer anointing and into the blessings of Psalm 24.

An idol can be rooted in vanity, pride, or the worship and adoration of anything other than God that has found a place in our heart. Our church can be an idol, your pastor can be an idol to you, your cars or home can become an idol to you, prophets and the adoration of prophetic ministries can become idols to you. One of the things that will hinder us from stepping into this realm of ascending into the hill of the Lord is idolatry and tolerating idols to reign in our heart.

Ezekiel talks about this. I would encourage you to read Ezekiel 13 and 14. Ezekiel 14:4 says, *"For anyone of the house of Israel, or of the strangers who dwell in Israel* [prophetically the Church]*, who separates himself from Me and sets up his idols in his heart and puts before him what causes him to stumble into iniquity, then comes to a prophet to inquire of him concerning Me, I the* Lord *will answer him by Myself."* There are times when gifts of the Spirit may become idols in our spirit and in our heart. I pray that you would read my book *Unlocking the Hidden Mysteries of the Seer Anointing*, where I talk about this dynamic in more detail. We need to search our hearts to make sure that we have clean hands pure hearts.

The fourth key that we see in Psalm 24:4 is *"nor sworn deceitfully."* This is another Hebraism, which means to swear or to take an oath with the words of your mouth; usually the Hebrew tradition was to say a thing seven times. We have to be careful with the words of our mouth. Remember, Jesus said in Matthew 12:36-37 that we will be judged by the words that come out of our mouth; *"By your words you will be justified, and by your words you will be condemned."* So, we need to be careful that we don't have a deceitful mouth or a deceitful spirit and we must be careful that we do not live our lives operating in a pattern of deception because of our tongue (James 3:6).

The Secrets of Our Hearts

It is possible to deceive other people. We can speak wittily or craftily and deceive other people. Sometimes we can even manage to deceive ourselves. But we cannot deceive God. God knows these things; He knows when we have deceitfulness within our spirit. God knows the secrets of our hearts. Remember the testimony that I shared about watching Jesus search the hearts of the people in the church in Springfield, Newfoundland? The Lord recognizes these things and will not allow us to step into the deeper things of God. He will not allow us to step into the greater levels that are available to us today of the seer realms or the seer anointing. I would encourage you to take some time and search your heart. Pray the prayer at the end of this chapter and ask the Holy Spirit to search your heart.

We need to recognize these four keys of Psalm 24:4 to release the blessings of Psalm 24 so we can begin to walk in those supernatural blessings. They come from one place; they come from the heavenly realms. We see that in scripture in Ephesians 1:3: *"Blessed be the God and Father of our Lord Jesus Christ, who has blessed us with every spiritual blessing in the heavenly places in Christ."* There are spiritual blessings that we can only receive from God in the heavenly places. They are rarely available in the earthly realms; but they are always available in the heavenly places.

One of the ways we can step into this supernatural grace which comes from these blessings is through understanding the blessings available to us spoken of in Psalm 24. Verse 5 tells us: *"He shall receive blessing from the LORD, And righteousness from the God of his salvation* [Jehovah].*"* Again, this is a twofold blessing. We could call this a double portion or a double anointing. I call this characteristic the double anointing of Psalm 24; the unmerited blessing of the Lord God Jehovah. God just pours His blessing upon us. He makes His face to shine upon you and all that is in your sphere of influence.

When I first got born again, I used to pray the prayer of Jabez in 1 Chronicles 4:10: *"Oh, that You would bless me indeed."* I was asking Jehovah to bless me; I was asking God the Father to bless me. And do you know what? He did. But there are other blessings that we can tap into when we recognize that we have the ability to access the hill of the Lord, which are the spiritual dimensions or realms. They are not available in the earthly realms; they are only available in the heavenly places. Remember, heaven is not always up; sometimes heaven comes down upon us.

I believe Psalm 24 is talking about the blessing of the Father—that the Father pours out His blessing upon your life. You could say that the supernatural favor of the Lord rests upon you as it did with Abraham or Jacob. So we could rightly say that an aspect of the anointing of Psalm 24 is just simply having the blessings of Abraham manifest in your life. Everything you put your hand to prospers. It's a wonderful thing! And it can be released from the Kingdom of Heaven.

Prayer for the Cleansing of the Heart (Based on Psalm 51)

Father, today in the mighty name of Jesus Christ of Nazareth, I ask You, Lord, that You would search my heart. Lord, search my inner parts; and through the power and ministry of the precious Holy Spirit, I ask that You would reveal anything that is hidden in the chambers of my heart. Lord, shine the light of Your Kingdom upon me and uncover any hidden agendas or hidden sins that I am not aware of. Lord, reveal any idols that I have unwittingly allowed to reign in my heart. Lord, I ask that You would heal and deliver me right now, in the name of Jesus Christ. Lord, I pray that You would minister to me according to the precepts of Psalm 51. Lord Jesus, wash me thoroughly from my iniquity and cleanse me from my sin. I acknowledge my transgressions, and my sin is always before me. Against You, You only, O Lord, have I sinned, and done evil in Your sight. Lord, may You be found just when You speak and blameless when You judge me, O God.

You are a merciful God. Remember, O Lord, that I was brought forth in iniquity and in sin my mother conceived me. Reveal Your truth and Your nature in my inward parts, and in the hidden parts may You allow me to know wisdom. Purge me with hyssop, and I shall be clean. Wash me with the blood of Jesus and I shall be whiter than snow. Make me hear with joy and gladness that even my bones may rejoice in You alone, Lord. Hide Your face from my sins, and blot out all my iniquities. And I pray in the name of Jesus that You would create in me a clean heart, O God, and renew a steadfast spirit within me. Cast me not away from Your presence, and do not take Your Holy Spirit from me. Lord, I ask that You restore to me the fullness of the joy of Your salvation, and uplift and heal me by the power of Your generous Spirit. Amen!

Now take some time to rest in the Lord and ask Him to speak to you One-to-one as a man does with his friend. If the Holy Spirit reveals any issues hidden within your heart or any other areas that you may need to repent for, just quietly repent before Him. And be assured that if we confess our sins, He is faithful and just to forgive us our sins and to cleanse us from all unrighteousness (1 John 1:9).

Now that you have prepared your hearts to receive the blessing of the Lord, let's continue to unlock the hidden blessings of Psalm 24 in the next chapter.

CHAPTER 15

Blessing I Will Bless You

I want to share a scriptural example of an individual upon the earth accessing the hill of the Lord or ascending to the hill of the Lord. Let's look at Genesis 22. Verse 15 says, *"Then the Angel of the LORD called to Abraham a second time out of heaven."* Where? Out of the hill of the Lord. This is an example of an open heaven and an example of the spiritual DNA that Abraham carried. He had the grace and favor of God upon his life. One of those blessings was that the proximity and presence of God was always upon him. Abraham was a glory carrier.

Abraham always had the pleasure of ascending to the hill of the Lord at the right time and in the right place (chronological and geographical obedience), where God would release supernatural blessings from the heavenly realms into his life. Abraham released that same blessing into his son Jacob (another Jewish tradition). God can use an individual to release a spiritual blessing into your life. Actually, it is a Hebrew custom and a Jewish family tradition. The father blesses the son. Your heavenly Father also has supernatural blessings to release to you as a son or daughter of the Most High God today.

In verses 16-17 of Genesis 22 we read that the angel of the Lord continued to speak to Abraham: "*By Myself I have sworn, says the* LORD, *because you have done this thing, and have not withheld your son, your only son—blessing I will bless you, and multiplying I will multiply you.*" Saying the words twice mean a double blessing or double anointing; it's part of the blessing of Abraham. It's part of getting the seer anointing activated in your life. Because when you get the seer anointing activated in your life, you can ascend to the hill of the Lord. And when you are mounting the hill of the Lord, God can speak such blessings over your life. You can receive a double portion.

It is also possible for God to employ other people to release these blessings into your life, when they have the spiritual authority to do so. Many of us miss this kind of blessing because we do not discern the true spiritual authority that God has placed upon the people around us. A good example of this could be Daisy in the previous testimony. I could have brushed her off and ignored her. But I discerned the anointing of the Holy Spirit that I caught in her eyes; as a result I received a blessing from the Lord by her words and generosity.

The Father's Blessing

We must discern who God will use to release the blessing of the Lord into our lives at times. I can point to a specific day in Jerusalem when Sid Roth laid hands upon me and spoke a father's blessing over my life. There was a marked increase in the grace and favor of God upon me after Sid prayed for me. Today we call this impartation. Actually, it is a Hebrew custom. Jesus most likely received a blessing from His earthly father,

Joseph, and He certainly received a blessing from His heavenly Father (Luke 3:22; Matthew 17:5).

Continuing with Genesis 22, verse 17, we read, "*I will multiply your descendants as the stars of the heaven and as the sand which is on the seashore; and your descendants shall possess the gate of their enemies.*" What's that? That is the ability to ascend to a place of judgment. This is not talking about the gates of Jerusalem. It is true that there were places near the gates in Jerusalem where there would be trials and there would be judgment that was passed. But in my opinion, this is talking about the gates that are in Mount Zion (heaven). This is talking about spiritual gates. These are some of the secrets found in Psalm 24. We *will* possess the gates of our enemy, the evil one. I believe God is raising up gatekeepers at this hour who will have the spiritual authority to open up gates in the spiritual realm. Why? So that people can ascend to the hill of the Lord to receive the blessings from God.

Genesis 22 continues in verse 18: "*In your seed all the nations of the earth shall be blessed, because you have obeyed My voice.*" This is the same root word for blessing that we see in Psalm 24. By implication it means to receive adoration, to receive favor, or to receive blessing directly from Jehovah. Do you want that? We can have it today. It's not something unobtainable for us. When we walk with clean hands and a pure heart; when we walk in holiness; when we choose to keep our spirit, soul, and mind focused on God and hear His voice and then see what He is asking us to do and are obedient to do those things; then we can ascend to the hill of the Lord and we will receive the blessing of God our Father. I am writing about seeing and hearing in a new way; it is a new paradigm.

Seek God

Psalm 24:6 reveals another key to releasing the blessings of Psalm 24: *"This is Jacob, the generation of those who seek Him, Who seek Your face."* We need to seek God's face. We need to seek His presence. We need to seek to be with Him. This is not because we need a *thing*, not because we want to be empowered, not because we need something; we just want to spend time with Him. I call it resting in the glory. We just want to come into His presence to be with Him. This is not to intercede, not to ask for anointing for a ministry need, not to ask for money for another ministry project. We just want to seek Him to be in His presence. So who may ascend to the hill of the Lord? You can!

We were doing a School of the Seers near Moravian Falls. I had been teaching for about ten hours over three days and I was tired. I went up into the hotel room in between sessions just to relax and rest. I just wanted to be with the Lord. As I was just lying there, I wasn't expecting anything. I just had forty-five or fifty minutes, and I just wanted to rest my feet and to be with God. Suddenly I was taken up into heaven and I came before the throne. I could hear all of heaven worshiping God. I had been in this place before. I looked to see Jesus standing there at my left hand. He was smiling at me. I thought, "Oh, this is awesome!"

Suddenly I heard the Father speak in a very loud voice, and the words "Come here; come up here" thundered throughout the throne room. It seemed that all of heaven and earth shook at that instant! I was looking around wondering, "Who is He talking to?" Then I realized, "He's talking to me!" You see, I had been caught up to that place before. I was startled when the Father reached out of the glory and took me in His mighty hands and pulled me into the intense phosphorescent glory that swirls around His throne.

The Father began to speak to me. One thing He told me was, "Kevin, I like it when you come before My throne of mercy and grace. Because when you come here, you don't come here and ask for things; you don't come here and seek judgment; you just come here and thank Me for what I do in your life. You just come here because you just want to be with Me. Then He just held me in the glory near His bosom for about another thirty-five minutes. The Lord spoke several other things into my spirit. These are of a personal nature, and I feel that it would be inappropriate to write about them here. Then He just set me back down beside the Lord. I turned to see Jesus smiling at me.

My spirit began to quake, and the next thing I knew I was translated back in the hotel room and found myself resting upon the bed. I thought, "Oh, I've got to get up and go teach the next session of the School of the Seers." So I went in the bathroom to brush my teeth. As I looked in the mirror, I discovered that about 25 percent of my hair had turned white. The first thing that happened when I walked into the meeting to teach was that somebody stopped me and said, "Your hair's white!" It was amazing. Thank the Lord it is now turning back to my natural color!

So who may ascend to the hill of the Lord? Those who have clean hands and a pure heart. But, just wanting to be with God, when we just hope to seek and *see* His face, is a key to activating this type of anointing in our lives. *We learned this in Israel.*

We need to seek the Lord while there is an opportunity to find Him (Isaiah 55:6). I believe we are living in a day and an hour when the passage of scripture in Psalm 24 can take on a whole new dynamic and meaning *if* you can believe to receive. If you don't believe God can take you up into the throne room and pull you into the glory, then it's probably not going to happen for you (Mark 16:17). But these kinds of miracles, signs, and wonders can follow and happen in your life! You *can* ascend to the hill of Jehovah.

Prayer of the Father's Blessing

Father, You promised to bless us with every blessing in the heavenly places. And today, heavenly Father, I ask that You would pour out upon me a Father's blessing. Father, in Jesus' name I pray that You would open the windows of heaven and release Your good treasure to me. Pour out Your grace and favor upon my life. It is Your good pleasure to give me the Kingdom; and today, Lord, I am asking that the Kingdom of Heaven would come upon my life in a fresh and new way. O Father, I ask that you would bless me indeed! Amen.

You can ascend to the habitation of God. One of the ways it's going to happen is to get the seer anointing activated and begin to walk in it with maturity of character. In the next chapter we will discover why you have already been prepared to ascend to the hill of the Lord and into the very presence of the King of Glory! *Praise you Jesus* ♡

CHAPTER 16

Ascending to the Hill of the Lord

I believe that we actually can ascend to the hill of the Lord (the mountain or habitation of Jehovah). I believe that we can actually go into the heavenly realms to obtain spiritual blessings—the blessings to be found in Christ. Why? Because Jesus, the King of Glory, has made a supernatural way for us. The Lord shed His blood to make you and me kings and priests to minister to our God and Father in the heavenly dimensions or heavenly realms.

We can literally go boldly behind the veil to see and hear what our heavenly Father is doing. I believe that we are living in a day and an hour that we must see and hear what God is doing. God will not withhold secrets from His friends. God will tell us where we need to be and when we need to be there. He will show us things that we need to do. Do you want to experience life like that? I do.

Let me show this to you. Look at Revelation 1:5-6: *"Jesus Christ, the faithful witness, the firstborn from the dead, and the ruler over the kings of the earth* [the terrestrial realm]. *To Him who loved us* [with God's apostolic love] *and washed us from our sins in His own blood, and has made us kings and priests to His God and Father, to Him be glory and dominion forever and ever."* Who are we supposed to minister to? God the Father. Where's God the Father? He's in the heavenly realms. It's the same Jehovah that Psalm 24 talks about in verse 3: *"Who may ascend into the hill of the LORD?"* Who may ascend to the habitation of Jehovah? Who may ascend into the presence of God? Every Christian; because the blood of Jesus has made us kings and priests.

It is a done deal. This is your inheritance given to you by the King. The finished work of Calvary makes you righteous and holy, and you can ascend to the hill of the Lord.

We see this again in Revelation 5:7-9: *"Then He came and took the scroll out of the right hand of Him who sat on the throne. Now when He had taken the scroll, the four living creatures and the twenty-four elders fell down before the Lamb, each having a harp, and golden bowls full of incense, which are the prayers of the saints. And they sang a new song, saying: 'You are worthy to take the scroll, And to open its seals; For You were slain, And have redeemed us to God by Your blood Out of every tribe and tongue and people and nation.'"*

So, why has the blood of God redeemed us? You see it in verse 10: to make *"us kings and priests to our God; And we shall reign on the earth"*—the terrestrial realm. The key is that the blood of Jesus makes a way for us to access the hill of the Lord in the spiritual realm. We see and hear what God is doing, and then we do those things just like Jesus did in John 5:19 in the earthly realm. We see and hear differently.

Psalm 24:7 tells us to *"lift up your heads, O you gates! And be lifted up, you everlasting doors! And the King of glory shall come in."* This passage gives us some additional keys to ascend to the hill of the Lord and to access the heavenly places.

Shaking the Space and Time Continuum

There are some amazing spiritual blessings in this passage of scripture which I had never seen before until February 25, 2014. On that day I had an angelic visitation in Moravian Falls, which I'll tell in more detail later. I had not seen these spiritual blessings during the twelve years that I had been reading this passage consistently because the Lord told us to name the ministry King of Glory Ministries International. The Lord spoke to me on March 13, 2002, in an audible voice and said to read Psalm 24 and base the ministry upon it. It was not until twelve years later I got this revelation on it. Why? Because this is the day and the hour that God is giving us eyes to see and ears to hear the heavenly truths that we could not comprehend before.

I believe there are things available to you that you would not have been able to understand even two weeks ago. That's the day and hour we live in. I believe you are reading this book by God's ordained timing, not by mistake. There is an acceleration in the spirit as the day of the Lord draws near.

Back to Psalm 24:7: *"Lift up your heads."* The actual language here means to be taken away, to rise up, or to be taken away in a supernatural manner in the same way as we learned from the previous passages of scripture. At this point it starts to get interesting. When I experienced the angelic visitation, on February 25, 2014, I believe the Lord gave me another revelation or understanding of the meaning of this passage. "*Your heads*" here in the original language means to shake the head (as in a ruler), to shake time, or to shake or motivate a captain or ruler. It is possible that as King David was writing this Psalm, he was releasing a profound mystery.

I believe that there are strong angels of God who have power and authority over time and who can open or close spiritual gates. I call these types of angels of God angels of supernatural provision or angels of creative miracles. Perhaps they are a type of archangel? These kinds of Godly angels can also be called gatekeepers. I believe that God is busy at this hour raising up people within the Body of Christ who will be mature, who will walk in a high level of the seer anointing, and who will discern these types of angelic gatekeepers. They will be given the liberty to co-labor with them to open and close spiritual gates. Angels of supernatural provision or angels of creative miracles can literally shake the space and time continuum. Daniel might be considered an individual who co-labored or minister with this type of angelic gate keeper (Daniel 10).

When this happens we can move backwards in time or we can move forwards in time. We can step into other Godly dimensions to obtain the blessings of the Lord. We can discern spiritual gates or portals of glory and position ourselves to receive the blessings of the Lord. When the space and time continuum shifts, the material (very subatomic structure) of objects can be shifted and change to God's preordained shape and makeup. That is why so many creative miracles happen in the glory realms.

The Anointing to Shake Time and Open Spiritual Gates

When the blessings of God (Jehovah) come upon our lives, we learn to walk in holiness and purity. At times we come into a grace and anointing like we see here in Psalm 24 to shake time and to have the favor of the Lord upon us to open or close spiritual gates or portals of glory. We have just seen examples of this in Genesis and in 2 Corinthians in the lives of Abraham, Jacob, and Paul the Apostle.

As we continue to look at Psalm 24:7, we see *"O you gates!"* This refers to an opening, a door, or a portal. *"Your heads, O Ye gates"* here is often taught incorrectly, in my opinion. At times people teach that this phrase refers to gates like the gates in Jerusalem or our eye gates or ear gates, and it *can* mean those things. But there could be other ways that this scripture can be interpreted.

These kinds of gates are spiritual gates and are not always open. I believe that God, Jehovah, has preordained times to open up or to close spiritual gates like these to allow His friends to ascend to the hill of the Lord or the heavenly dimensions or the Godly dimensions.

There are gates or portals that open up into heavenly dimensions or Godly dimensions; but there are also gates and portals that open up into evil or demonic dimensions. That puts a whole new meaning upon the key of David. I believe that when Jesus said in Matthew 16:19 that *"I will give you the keys of the kingdom of heaven, and whatever you bind on earth will be bound in heaven, and whatever you loose on earth will be loosed in heaven,"* He was also referring to closing, locking, and binding gates that open and close into the demonic dimensions. I believe that Jesus literally gave His friends the authority to close the gates of hell and to stop evil and nefarious schemes from occurring.

Let's look at this in Isaiah 22:22: *"The key of the house of David I will lay on his shoulder."* What that means is that the Lord will appoint or give authority to use such a key. *"He shall open, and no one shall shut."* The literal language here means He shall set free. The verse continues: *"And he shall shut, and no one shall open."* This means to plug up or stop. So, when God releases the key of David into someone's life, He is giving them spiritual authority to open up gates that no man can close and to close gates that no man can open.

Why can't a man open them? Because they are spiritual gates and you need delegated spiritual authority to use the keys to unlock them. I believe this is the day and hour that we live in: God is releasing to His friends the authority to see and hear into the spiritual realm and to discern when these spiritual gates are open so we can step into them to receive blessings and revelation. On the other hand God can also use His friends to lock, close, or to plug up gates into demonic realms to thwart the plans of the enemy.

Be Lifted Up and Be Blessed

When these kinds of portals or doors are open in the heavenly dimensions, there is a grace and favor of the Lord that is released into an individual's life just like we saw in the life of Abraham and Jacob. God can do these same things today. When God opens up Godly gates in spiritual dimensions, Jehovah can

Ascending to the Hill of the Lord

release spiritual blessings into our lives. I believe that God can release amazing spiritual blessings and anointing into your life and into your sphere of influence at this hour.

Continuing on in Psalm 24:7, it says, "*And be lifted up.*" This is the same language used before in Psalm 24:3 where it says, "*Ascend into the hill of the LORD.*" We can be lifted up by God into the spiritual realms. Back to verse 7, we ask, what is to be lifted up? "*You everlasting doors!*" The language here actually refers to an opening, a door, a gate, an entranceway, or an entrance point. This is speaking of doors or gates into the spiritual realms. It actually can be translated as a vanishing point. You are in this dimension one moment and you are in the heavenly realms the next. One instant you are here in the terrestrial realm and the next second you are in the heavenly realms or dimensions.

Prayer of Covering

Lord Jesus, thank You for Your blood. I cover myself in Your blood right now, and I thank You that Your blood is the most powerful substance upon the earth. Thank You, *Lord, for washing me and totally forgiving me from by sins with Your own blood. Lord Jesus, today I recognize that by the power of Your blood, I have been transformed into a king and royal priest. And I thank You, Lord, that these privileges open up the doors and gates of the heavenly realms and make a way for me to minister to my God and Father. Thank You, Lord Jesus, because You have redeemed us to God by Your blood. Thank You, Lord, that I may ascend into the hill of the Lord. As I mature and learn to walk in greater levels of holiness and purity each day, I ask that You would give me further revelation of what it means to bind on earth and that I might also learn how to loose Your kingdom upon the earth and understand the mysteries of what will be loosed in heaven. In Jesus' name I pray. Amen.*

These are hidden mysteries, I believe, that God is releasing to His friends at this hour through the seer realm. God's friends will begin to see and hear and discern these types of hidden mysteries in God's Kingdom. And I believe these are keys in Psalm 24 that are available to us today that might not have been available to us two years ago or even two weeks ago. It is the King of Glory who allows His friends to have this type of Kingdom authority. Let's continue to learn more of the hidden mysteries about these spiritual gates of open heavens in the next chapter. We are going to move away from our discoveries in Psalm 24 and begin to look at other spiritual principles concerning these kinds of spiritual gates of breakthrough and blessing.

CHAPTER 17

The Double Doors of Breakthrough

I believe that it is the season when the Lord of Hosts, the King of Glory is actively opening the double doors and double gates of breakthrough. We have entered into a season for the blessings of Psalm 24 to be poured out. The year 2014 on our Gregorian calendar is the year of break though and the year of the double door on the Hebrew calendar. It is the Hebrew year of 5774, meaning an open door of breakthroughs (2 Samuel 5:20). In 2014 the Lord opened the double doors of breakthrough that will never close again.

There are times when a door in heaven is actively opening. We see an example of this in Revelation 4:1: *"After these things I looked, and behold, a door standing open in heaven."* This is an amazing passage of scripture. The language here seems to indicate that the Apostle John witnessed, discerned, or saw a door that was actively opening. This gate or door then allowed John to access or ascend into the hill of the Lord and receive the revelation that constitutes the entire Book of Revelation.

The point that I want to make is that at God-ordained times the Lord has ordained for spiritual doors or gates into the heavenly dimensions to be active and open to allow free access into the heavenly dimensions. We have entered into such a season. In my opinion the double doors and gates of breakthrough that the Lord is actively opening in this time will never shut again. The Lord is giving His friends the freedom to move about the heavenly dimensions as never before!

When God begins to open spiritual gates and doors like this, there are scriptural blessings and anointing that are released to God's friends. I want to look at these movements of the heavenly realms (the anointing and blessings of Psalm 24) into the terrestrial realms or earthly dimensions. It can be "on earth as it is in heaven" (Matthew 6:10) in your life as you learn to discern these kinds of double doors and gates of breakthrough.

The Lord dropped these passages of scripture into my heart to share with you concerning spiritual gates and heavenly doors. In fact, as I was working on this, I had an encounter with the Holy Spirit where I felt He breathed upon them. The Lord is speaking through Isaiah the prophet in the following passages. Let's read Isaiah 45:1-8:

> *Thus says the LORD to His anointed, To Cyrus, whose right hand I have held—To subdue nations before him And loose the armor of kings, To open before him the double doors, So that the gates will not be shut: "I will go before you And make the crooked places straight; I will break in pieces the gates of bronze And cut the bars of iron. I will give you the treasures of darkness And hidden riches of*

secret places, That you may know that I, the LORD, *Who call you by your name, Am the God of Israel. For Jacob My servant's sake, And Israel My elect, I have even called you by your name; I have named you, though you have not known Me. I am the* LORD, AND THERE IS NO OTHER; THERE IS NO GOD BESIDES ME. I WILL GIRD YOU, THOUGH YOU HAVE NOT KNOWN ME, THAT THEY MAY KNOW FROM THE RISING OF THE SUN TO ITS SETTING THAT THERE IS NONE BESIDES ME. I AM THE LORD, AND THERE IS NO OTHER; I FORM THE LIGHT AND CREATE DARKNESS, I MAKE PEACE AND CREATE CALAMITY; I, THE LORD, DO ALL THESE THINGS.' RAIN DOWN, YOU HEAVENS, FROM ABOVE, AND LET THE SKIES POUR DOWN RIGHTEOUSNESS; LET THE EARTH OPEN, LET THEM BRING FORTH SALVATION, AND LET RIGHTEOUSNESS SPRING UP TOGETHER. I, THE LORD, HAVE CREATED IT.

I believe this is the season that we are in. God is releasing the blessings of Psalm 24 and He is opening up the gates and doors of heaven to allow us to ascend into the hill of the Lord. It's the season of Deuteronomy 28:12 where God is releasing to His people His good treasure of the open heavens. And when God opens the gates and doors of heavens over our lives, the blessings of the heavenly realms, the blessings of Jehovah, rain down upon us.

The Season of the Rain of Revival

I believe it's the season of the fresh latter rains. I believe it's the season of the rain of revival and advancement of the Kingdom of Heaven. I believe that we have stepped into a time when God is going to open up gates and doors in heaven and that there are going to be blessings poured out upon our lives. I believe that the Lord is releasing and opening up some of these kinds of supernatural double doors, gates of breakthrough, and the windows of heaven to His people. They were not available a year ago or even two months ago or perhaps even two weeks ago. I believe this is a new thing the Lord is doing.

Let's go back through this passage of scripture. In Isaiah 45:1 it starts out: *"Thus says the LORD."* "Lord" in this place means Jehovah, Father, God Almighty. The verse continues: *"To His anointed."* The word translated "anointed" is a Hebrew word that is the root word for Messiah. Usually it means a consecrated person, a king, a priest, or a saint. (I believe we are living in a day and an hour that God is raising up a royal priesthood according to the order of Melchizedek spoken of in Hebrews 7:17. I believe we are all called to be transformed into the image of Jesus; we are all called to be God's anointed). There is a lot of hidden revelation concealed in this verse.

Isaiah 45:1 continues by identifying who this anointed one is whom Father is addressing: *"To Cyrus, whose right hand I have held."* This is a Hebraism in this passage of scripture when the prophet Isaiah talks in this manner. What he is saying is that to hold the right hand, to hold the leg, or to hold the eye of a person means to be held in a position of security by one who is stronger or who has more power or is more powerful. It can also mean to be protected by one who is more skillful in battle than you are. It means to be held or helped by the right hand of God. It means to rest in the Lord and allow Him to work upon your behalf or to hold your right hand. Learn to allow

Jehovah to hold your "little hands." Mothers and fathers have experienced times when your children were toddlers and you held them by their little hands; that is a picture of what this passage is speaking about.

When we allow God to hold our hand, we are really allowing God to lead us as if we were that small child. This is not a posture of weakness; this is a posture of submission—a meekness that is in no way related to weakness. When we submit to God and allow Him to hold our right hand, we are meek in the way Jesus referred to in Matthew 5:5: *"Blessed are the meek, For they shall inherit the earth."* Some interpret this as being weak, but that is not what the Lord meant. It means to be humble, to be spiritually pure, or to be God-minded. Remember these are some of the same supernatural keys that unlock the blessings of Psalm 24 that we learned earlier. They confirm this spiritual principle.

So when we submit to God and allow Him to hold our right hand, we are becoming more Christlike. Our mind is being transformed into the mind of Christ. It means to allow Jehovah to hold our right hand. It speaks of resting in God and allowing the Lord God Almighty—the Lord of Israel, Jehovah—to battle on our behalf. We rest in God and then the Lord works. We rest, God works. When Jesus cried out on the Cross, "It is finished" (John 19:30), His work was done. The Lord no longer labors. He is seated at the right hand of the Father. He has entered into the rest of the Lord that we see in Hebrews 4. He intercedes for you from that place of Kingly power and authority.

The Kingly Anointing

God is calling His people to quit laboring and to be diligent to enter into His rest (Hebrews 4:11). From a place of rest, God will work on our behalf. That is what this passage of scripture in Isaiah 45 is describing. We learn to ascend into the hill of the Lord to see and hear in a new way. We discern and discover the intercessory prayers of Jesus as He is seated at the right hand of the Father. Then we simply do those same things that we see and hear our Lord doing and miraculous things happen in our lives and sphere of influence. This anointing to see and to hear in a new way is activated when we learn to discern these kinds of supernatural gates and double doors Isaiah is describing.

We see next in Isaiah 45:1 that God begins to war on our behalf. We see this dynamic outlined for us: "To subdue nations before him And loose the armor of kings." The language here has a specific meaning. It means the loins or the riches of kings. The Hebrew word translated "kings" is melekh. I told you that God is calling you to be a royal priest according to the order of Melchizedek. Melchizedek was the king of peace or the king of Salem. When we begin to realize our God-ordained destiny to step into this type of royal priesthood to become kings and priests of queens and priestesses according to the order of Melchizedek, it's not some farfetched theology. Simply, what it means is that we become transformed into the very image of Jesus.

Jesus Christ is our role model for this type of kingly anointing. It's an anointing to open up spiritual gates and spiritual doors. I will touch on that later as we pray to step through spiritual gates to release breakthroughs from the heavenly realms into our lives in the natural realm. By reading this you can access these blessings of Jehovah or the Father. It is the same kind of anointing that we have seen in Psalm 24. Jesus gives His friends the keys to open and close these kinds of spiritual gates (Matthew 16:19).

When the scripture says *"the armor of kings"* in Isaiah 45:1, it is speaking of fortified doors, heavily fortified doors at the stronghold where kings have storehouses of riches and treasures. God wants to give those hidden riches to you. Let's look at this dynamic in a little bit more detail in the Book of Hebrews. Although I will just touch on it here, I encourage you to read the book *The Sword of the Lord and the Rest of the Lord*, where I talk about it in great detail.

Beginning with verse 14 of Hebrews 4, the writer is speaking of allowing God to work on our behalf as we learn to rest in Him: *"Seeing then that we have a great High Priest who has passed through the heavens."* Jesus accessed the doors or gates of heaven; He went (and continues to pass) *"behind the veil"* (Hebrews 6:19). "Behind the veil" is another Hebraism, which means to enter into the very presence of God or literally into heaven. Jesus, as our Forerunner, has blazed a trail for us to follow in His footsteps. In this way Jesus perfectly illustrates the Psalm 24 paradigm.

Going on with Hebrews 4, verse 14 we read, *"Jesus the Son of God, let us hold fast our confession."* Praise God! We have a confession we can hold fast to. What is it? Number one, it is impossible for God to lie to us (Hebrews 6:18). And number 2, we have a Forerunner (v. 20), Jesus Christ of Nazareth, who has entered into the heavenly realms, who has filled the Messianic prophesies, who has overcome the world, and who has sat down at the right hand of the Father where He is now resting from His work. We are to emulate that character of Christ; we are to emulate Jesus in this regard at this hour. We are to cease from our works. We are to allow Jehovah to hold our hand and work on our behalf. Then we see and hear from the heavenly realms what God has ordained for us to walk in and it unfolds in a supernatural fashion.

Prayer for Discernment of Spiritual Gates

Lord, I ask, in the mighty name of Jesus Christ, for You to open my spiritual eyes. Lord, help me to discern the prayers of Jesus. Father, I ask that You would give me the grace to discern the spiritual gates that You have ordained for me to perceive. Help me to ascend into the hill of the Lord. Lord, help me to position myself correctly at Your spiritual gates to release breakthroughs from the heavenly realms into my life in the natural realm. Lord, help me to access the blessings of Jehovah from Your word in my life today. Lord, I ask in Jesus' name that You would activate the double anointing and the blessings of Psalm 24 in my life. Lord Jesus, release the revelation and the keys into my life to open and close the spiritual gates around me. And, Lord, I ask for wisdom and revelation of the times and season to do these things. In Jesus' name I pray. Amen.

We can learn to pass through heavenly realms to access the hill of the Lord as we have seen in Psalm 24. This is possible because of the finished work of Calvary. We can emulate Jesus' example. In the next chapter we will learn how to access this promise of the kingly anointing and this same type of inheritance that the Lord has already given to you.

CHAPTER 18

Enter the Presence Behind the Veil

Hebrews 6:17-18 continues to further unlock these mysteries for us: *"Thus God, determining to show more abundantly to the heirs of promise the immutability of His counsel, confirmed it by an oath, that by two immutable things, in which it is impossible for God to lie, we might have strong consolation, who have fled for refuge to lay hold of the hope set before us."* What hope do we have? It tells us as we go on to verse 19: *"This hope we have as an anchor of the soul, both sure and steadfast, and which enters the Presence behind the veil."*

We've touched on this: "the veil" is a Hebraism, which means to enter in through a thinly spread veil, to enter into a door. In Hebrew culture this phrase meant to enter into the most holy place—referring to the veil in the Jewish temple that separated the outer court and the inner court from the Holy of Holies, a very sacred place where God dwelt. God is opening up doors which will allow His friends to move freely about the heavenly realms without fear. You can move from the outer court into His glory and into the Holy of Holies.

That veil, by the way, is believed by many theologians to be four to six inches thick and about twenty to twenty-two feet tall. The veil of the temple was thought to be a beautiful purple color. When the high priest entered through the veil once a year on the Day of Atonement, they would often tie a rope to his ankle. They would listen for bells that were fastened to the hem of the priestly robe to determine if he was still alive. If they didn't hear the bells, they could pull him out by the rope around his ankle. Before the finished work of Calvary, it was a fearful proposition to enter into the glory and presence of Almighty God.

Through the finished work of Jesus Christ, we have the liberty and the luxury of entering through the veil, passing behind the veil, passing into the heavenly realms, entering into the glory of God to see and hear what our Father is doing. Because of the blood of Jesus, we no longer have to fear dying when we come into His presence. That's good news! We enter into that place through supernatural gates and doors. These are open heavens.

Entering or going behind the veil is synonymous with entering into the heavenly realms. Going behind the veil is synonymous with ascending into the hill of the Lord. We no longer need to die to do that. Hebrews 6:20 goes on to tell us why that is: for we have a Forerunner who *"has entered for us, even Jesus, having become High Priest forever according to the order of Melchizedek."* So what hope is set before us? The hope of passing through the heavens and entering into the *"Presence behind the veil"* (v. 19). In the New King James and other translations "Presence" is capitalized, indicating entering in to the very presence or glory of Jehovah or God. And we can access the supernatural realms through supernatural doors or gates. This is your call. This is your mission as a royal priest according to the order of Melchizedek (5:9).

The Delegated Authority of God

This is the season that the Lord is accelerating this supernatural process. This is the season that the Lord is activating and releasing this spiritual principle in the Kingdom of God to whosoever will. This speaks of supernatural favor with both God and man. But I also believe it speaks of receiving spiritual authority in the heavenly realms and the grace to receive the blessings of Psalm 24. It speaks of being endued or graced with power and authority in the spiritual realm. The Lord can anoint or bless us with the grace gift or delegated authority of God to have power over demonic realms (Mark 6:7).

A good illustration of this point would be the story in Acts about the sons of Sceva. I believe God is raising up mature sons and daughters of God who have spiritual authority to open up doors in the Godly dimension and close doors that lead to ungodly dimensions. In the following passage of scripture, we see that as some Jewish exorcists were trying to cast out demons in the name of Jesus because they had seen others do it, they had an encounter with a demonic power. We read about this in Acts 19:13-15:

> *Then some of the itinerant Jewish exorcists took it upon themselves to call the name of the Lord Jesus over those who had evil spirits, saying, "We exorcise you by the*

> *Jesus whom Paul preaches." Also there were seven sons of Sceva, a Jewish chief priest, who did so. And the evil spirit answered and said, "Jesus I know, and Paul I know; but who are you?"*

This scripture illustrates an important fact and dynamic: in the spiritual realm, demonic entities *do* recognize those who carry or are endued with the authority of the Kingdom of God and, conversely, those who do not truly have legitimate spiritual authority. At this time God is raising up mature sons and daughters of God who *will* walk in the power of God and who *will* have *exousia* (authority) delegated in the spiritual realm (Luke 10:19; Matthew 28:18-20).

We have stepped into a God-ordained moment of time when the Lord is releasing this kind of supernatural authority to His friends to open up doors, to open up spiritual gates, and to open up portals of glory in the Psalm 24 model. I have a friend who came upon a portal that opened up and a fifty-carat gemstone fell from the heavenly realms. There has been a season where that has happened periodically in certain geographic places. But what if this dynamic could happen consistently in anyone's life? I believe we have stepped into that day. I believe we have stepped into that hour.

I believe there are supernatural gates, supernatural portals or windows into the spiritual dimensions that God is releasing for His friends to open and close. Sometimes the Lord will pour out gemstones from these windows. Remember the testimony that I shared about seeing Jesus pour out heavenly treasure into the meeting in Springdale, Newfoundland? We actually have a few of those kinds of supernatural gemstones. I took some supernatural amethysts that appeared from the heavenly dimensions and had an artist make a gold pendant for Kathy one holiday with those glory stones! Heaven is real!

Remember, there are Godly spiritual dimensions; but on the other hand, there are also spiritual gates into demonic dimensions. So, what we are talking about is having the authority to also bind evil plans and the nefarious schemes when they are released through open gates of darkness.

Let's review Matthew 16 because Jesus talked about this. Again, these scriptures illustrate a spiritual principle. Peter had just had an amazing revelation that Jesus Christ was, indeed, the Messiah. In verses 17-18 of Matthew 16 it says, *"Jesus answered and said to him, 'Blessed are you, Simon Bar-Jonah, for flesh and blood has not revealed this to you, but My Father who is in heaven. And I also say to you that you are Peter, and on this rock I will build My church, and the gates of Hades shall not prevail against it.'"*

The word translated "prevail" really means to open. What Jesus is really saying is, "Peter, I am giving you and the church authority (*kratos* power) to shut demonic gates or doors. Perhaps you have never seen that passage of scripture in this context before?

Continuing with verse 19, Jesus says, *"And I will give you the keys of the kingdom of heaven, and whatever you bind on earth will be bound in heaven, and whatever you loose on earth will be loosed in heaven."* What are keys for? Keys open and close doors, do they not? The Greek word translated "gates" in verse 18 can mean gates but is also similar to a plant or a flower opening and closing. Spiritual gates open and they close. Most gates do not remain open indefinitely; they open and then they close. This word can also be translated as a door that swings both ways. So when God opens a door in the heavenly realms, we can ascend or cross over or penetrate behind the veil and step into the heavenly realms. And the heavenly realms can also be poured out upon us. The Kingdom can move both ways, there is descending of blessings and favor and there can be ascending to receive more of the same!

Possess the Gates of Your Enemies

There are supernatural openings and spiritual gates like this. I don't believe this was something that was relegated to the Old Testament. I don't believe this was something that was relegated to the first century church. I believe that this is something that has always been part of the Kingdom of God. And I believe there is an acceleration of God releasing to His children, to His friends, spiritual authority to open and close spiritual doors today. The Lord wants His Bride, His church, to wake up and realize and to discern the power and authority that He has given us over spiritual gates. He wants us to understand that we can open and close these types of gates and these types of doors when He gives us His authority to do so. *We must tell you.*

When Jesus' body was buried in that unused grave, His Spirit was busy. He plundered hell. Look at what Jesus says in Revelation 1:18: *"I am He who lives, and was dead, and behold, I am alive forevermore. Amen. And I have the keys of Hades and of Death."* What do you think that Jesus is going to do with the keys to the gates of hell? He will permanently lock and block them! Jesus disarmed demonic powers and made a public spectacle of them, and by so doing He triumphed over them. Jesus possesses the gates of our enemies.

We see this aspect of the ministry of Jesus as He was passing through spiritual gates and going behind the veil outlined in Ephesians 4:8-13: Read

> *"When He [Jesus] ascended on high, [through gates], He led captivity captive, And gave gifts [or blessings] to men." (Now this, "He ascended"—what does it mean but that He also first descended, [through gates], into the lower parts of the earth? He who descended is also the One who ascended, [through gates], far above all the heavens, that He might fill all things.) And He Himself gave some to be apostles, some prophets, some evangelists, and some pastors and teachers, for the equipping of the saints for the work of ministry, for the edifying of the body of Christ, till we all come to the unity of the faith and of the knowledge of the Son of God, to a perfect man, to the measure of the stature of the fullness of Christ.*
> (Bracketed phrases added by author.)

This is exciting! Blessings are released to us when we discern the open gates or portals of heaven. I believe that this revelation can be life changing for you. Not only can you get the spiritual gates and the heavens opened up over your church and your city and your ministry, but you can get the heavens opened up over your individual life. As we have learned in Deuteronomy 28:12, it is God's good pleasure to give us the open heavens. Again, this is one of the blessings of Psalm 24. This is directly related to what Jesus said: *"I will give you the keys of the Kingdom of Heaven,"* You can learn to discern spiritual gates and you can also be empowered by the Lord to possess them as well!

The very first blessing that God gave to Abraham, as recorded in Genesis 22:17, came in such a place—where there was an open heaven, a Mahanaim or heavenly gate, on Mt. Moriah. Abraham received a blessing when he came to a geographical place where a gate or the gates of heaven were open. We have looked at the blessing God speaks over Abraham in Genesis 22, but I want to make sure you get the full revelation. Often a part of a scripture is shared and not the whole concept, so let's look at it in context. In Genesis 22:17 God Almighty is speaking to Abraham saying, *"Blessing I will bless you, and multiplying I will multiply your descendants as the stars of the Heaven and as the sand which is on the seashore; and your descendants shall possess the gate of their enemies."* Do you want to do that?

Many times theologians teach about the blessings of Abraham concerning prosperity and health, but one of the real benefits of having the blessings of Abraham activated in your life is getting the heavens open over your life so you possess the gates of your enemy. Let me submit to you that these are spiritual gates. In fact, the Hebrew word translated "possess" in Genesis 22 means to drive out with authority, to drive out with power, or to dispossess one's foe. Do you want to do that? Remember, in Jewish culture the gates were a place of judgment. So when God promises Abraham that he would possess the gates of his enemies, it means that God would give him the power to have judgment over his enemies. However, discerning spiritual gates can also be the key that unlocks supernatural prosperity in your life. You see, having the keys to the Kingdom of Heaven is directly related to the gates of hell not prevailing against us (Matthew 16:19).

In the next chapter we will begin to discover more of the hidden mysteries of supernatural gates and doors. It is possible for you to activate double doors of heavenly blessings over your life today.

Prayer to Possess the Gates of Your Enemies

Lord, I ask in the name of Jesus that You help me to understand the hidden mysteries of spiritual gates. Jesus, I ask that You give me eyes to see and a spirit to discern in a new way. Help me to recognize these spiritual principles and understand how to receive from the open heaven of Your Kingdom. Lord, also give me the wisdom and authority to close the doors of the enemy that open and are affecting my life. Lord, help me to discern and to possess the gates of my enemies. In Jesus' name I pray. Amen.

CHAPTER 19

Unlocking the Double Doors of Breakthrough

Going back to Isaiah 45, we realize there is a lot of hidden revelation in this chapter of scripture. As I sat in my office in Moravian Falls, the winds of heaven came in and God began to breathe upon this passage of scripture. I want to share this Pneuma (breath of God) with you as you read this book.

In Isaiah 45:1 we read, *"To open before him the double doors."* What that really means is two-leaved gates. This is not a regular way to open a gate. It means to open up wide—specifically to loosen, to plow, to carve, to make appear, to break forth or to break open wide, or to draw out. The meaning can also be translated as to let go free, to be set free (as in the gates of a prison), to loose or to set free, or to be in an open place or a place of blessing. It means to put off shackles or heavy burdens, to make unstoppable, to vent, or allow light to penetrate into a place. This perfectly describes the double blessing and the anointings of Psalm 24.

This is the season of the double door. This is the *kiaros* moment of time for the double gates of breakthrough and

143

victory to open over your life. God is going to allow the Body of Christ to possess the gates of our enemies as well. So when the Lord goes before us to open the gates or supernatural doors, it has a wonderful compound and supernatural connotation—multiple connotations. It speaks of the Lord God Jehovah opening up the spiritual realm (the open heavens) for you.

There is going to be a grace for impartation for open heavens. Just like the testimony that I shared about November 25, 2001, when I saw the heavens open and I saw Jesus descend into a small church in Springdale, Newfoundland, Canada. Ever since that time there's been a grace on my life. At times the Holy Spirit allows and releases me to deposit or to share that impartation with other people; people like you. I believe that grace is present upon this book for you to receive an impartation of open heavens. If you are reading this, you can receive the impartation even now!

The Great Banquet Hall

We must always remember that doors like this can only be discerned when the Lord reveals them to us. There are seasons and *kiaros* moments of time when the Lord releases His grace to us, empowering us to learn to discern spiritual gates and doors. Let me share a testimony with you about this kind of supernatural learning and discerning. When I was first saved, I would go to heaven (ascend to the hill of the Lord) almost every day for about nine months and I would fellowship with Jesus. My favorite place to go was the great banquet hall. I would just lay there at the feet of Jesus and absorb His glory. The great banquet hall is so beautiful and so big. Even the

Unlocking the Double Doors of Breakthrough

Dallas Cowboys' *AT&T Stadium* would be tiny in comparison to the great banquet hall. Tables are lined up with thousands and thousands of dinner settings already in place—the china, the crystal glasses, everything is ready for the wedding supper of the Lamb. I would go there and I would fellowship with Jesus. I have gone many, many, many times.

One day as I was fellowshipping with the Lord, He said, "Come with Me. I want to show you something." I thought, "Great! Maybe we are going to go to Psalm 23; maybe we're going to go to the still waters. Maybe we are going to go to the manicured gardens. Maybe we are going to go to the vineyard. Maybe we are going to go to the fountain of living waters!" I just love to go to all these different places in heaven with Jesus. If you would like to read about what heaven looks like, then read the book *Angels in the Realms of Heaven*.

But this day the Lord took me down along the wall of the great banquet hall. It looks kind of like a castle you might see in medieval times or perhaps a little like the Wailing Wall in Jerusalem. The walls are made of stones—beautiful, incredible craftsmanship with no seams between them. I have no idea how they could build it with no mortar or anything; the stones fit perfectly together. The Lord stopped at one point, looked at the wall, and said, "Look."

I looked and said, "Lord, I don't see anything." He said, "Look again." When I looked again the wall began to start to fade in and out like a mirage. Jesus was once more teaching me to see in a new way! Then I saw a door materialize in the stone as the eyes of my understanding were enlightened (Ephesians 1:18). Jesus was teaching and training me about the seer anointing again that day back in 2002. I believe that the Lord wanted me to share with you that discerning spiritual doors is the same as this. The Lord allowed me to watch as this door opened. The door led to a long pathway that ended in the throne room. We entered into the throne room and walked up to the stairs to the throne. Again, this was a vision within a vision. This experience was a Psalm 24 encounter.

The point I want to make is that God has to reveal these types of supernatural gates and these types of supernatural doors to you. And when this happens, when God releases you to see these things, God often releases into your life a supernatural blessing. There is a supernatural favor that comes from both God and man when you begin to walk in this type of discernment. I call it the seer anointing—when you begin to discern supernatural truths, when you begin to perceive spiritual gates.

You begin to pass behind the veil. As we learned, Jesus Christ is the royal Priest according to the order of Melchizedek and was the Forerunner who blazed the trail for us. When we follow our Forerunner behind the veil into spiritual realms through spiritual gates like this, there is a grace and favor; the fragrance of heaven attaches itself to you.

I believe for many of you reading this that you are in a God-ordained geographical location, a Mahanaim, at a God-ordained moment of time to receive a blessing from Almighty God. The anointing is like this, it's a double anointing and it's just like everything you touch prospers.

Continuing in Isaiah 45:1, we read, *"So that the gates will not be shut."* We touched on this in Psalm 24; we can ascend into

Paul Keith told us to read Is 45:1 all

the habitation of the Lord and shake the windows or doors of heaven and they will open. It's important for us to understand this verse: "*So that the gates will not be shut.*" The Hebrew word translated "gates" here is different than the word translated "two-leaved gates" or "double doors" we looked at earlier in the verse. The word translated "gates" here means an opening—for example, a door or a gate, specifically the gate to a strong or well guarded city or the gate to a fortified city or a fortified door; but it can also mean a gate or a port. Gates that cannot be shut offer free uninhibited access to the hill of the Lord or into the habitation of God.

Prayer to Be Truly Blessed and Highly Favored

Lord, I thank You that I am truly blessed and highly favored with great, great grace and divine intervention in my life today. I am a King's kid and a royal priest according to the order of Melchizedek, and I am walking in the FOG—the favor of God! Amen.

Today we might call supernatural gates like we find in Psalm 24 and Isaiah 45 portals of glory or open heavens. The thing I want you to see is that gates like this are continually open over some people's lives. Do you know some people that prosper no matter what happens?

Abraham lived under an open heaven after he was blessed by Melchizedek. Everything that he touched prospered. Some people are like that; if you give them lemons they make lemonade—it doesn't matter what happens in their life, it turns out they prosper from every circumstance. All things seem to work together for their good!

That's because they have this type of spiritual dynamic operating in their lives; they are living under an open heaven. The blessings and double anointing of Psalm 24 are continually in operation in their lives and also rest upon their generational line. Their children's children are truly blessed and highly favored, they just prosper (Genesis 22:16-18). In the next chapter we will seek to discover additional Kingdom keys that can help you to activate the blessings and double anointing of Psalm 24 in your life.

CHAPTER 20

Unlocking the Secret Gates of the Treasury

How do we get the heavens opened up over our lives? How do we activate the blessings of Psalm 24 in our lives? One example scriptural example would be found in Matthew 17 where Peter, James, and John were taken by Jesus to a specific geographical place (the Mount of Transfiguration) at a specific chronological time, and they saw Christ transfigured before them. Later in Acts 4:20 when Peter and John were in front of the Sanhedrin, who could well have crucified them, they said, *"We cannot but speak the things which we have seen and heard."*

When God opens up the realms of heaven over your life and you step into this dynamic, the Kingdom of Heaven becomes real to you. You begin to encounter the Kingdom consistently, and it can never be taken from you. You learn to taste the Kingdom, touch the Kingdom, feel the Kingdom, and, of course, hear and see the Kingdom in a new way! I believe you are going to experience a release of God's blessings and the double anointing of Psalm 24 to you as you read this book. God's favor, God's power can be poured out upon your life like a river. It can rain down continually to give you fruit in season and out of season. You can be like those trees planted by the river of God in Revelation 22, whose leaves are always blooming, always bearing fruit, touching the nations (v. 2).

It is important to remember that when we possess the gates of our enemies, we can stop them up, we can shut them; we can take the keys of the Kingdom of Heaven and lock gates or portals leading into the demonic realms as God empowers us. That eliminates the evil and the nefarious plans of the enemy from operating in your life and your sphere of influence. When you learn to discern demonic spiritual gates and shut them by the power and authority of the Holy Spirit, you will be set free from things like sickness, oppression, and poverty. On the other hand, we receive the blessings of the Lord when we discern gates into the Godly dimensions.

Places or gates of supernatural blessings like this can be called Mahanaims. In Genesis 32 we read of Jacob, who came to such a place. Jacob's spiritual DNA was to live under an open heaven because of his genealogical line. Your spiritual DNA is to live under an open heaven; because as born-again believers in this Man named Jesus, the Messiah, the Anointed One, you have been grafted into the tree of life. You have the same spiritual DNA as Jesus Christ of Nazareth; and therefore, you have the right to live your life under an open heaven like we see here in Genesis 32. Beginning with verses 1 and 2, we read, *"So Jacob went on his way, and the angels of God met him. When Jacob saw them."* Boom! What happens? The seer anointing activates in his life. He came to a place where the heavens were opened; and in that place of open heavens, his spiritual senses were activated so that he could see and hear from the heavenly realms. A Mahanaim is a door of the blessings like we see in Psalm 24.

In Luke 3:21-22 we read where Jesus came to John to be baptized. And the scripture says that while He was being baptized, they saw the Holy Spirit descend bodily in the form of a dove and they heard the voice of the Father saying, *"You are My beloved Son; in You I am well pleased"* (v. 22). What was that? That was an example of a Mahanaim. That was an example of the heavens opening up. That was an example of Deuteronomy 28:12. God opened up His good treasure, the heavens, and rained blessings down upon people.

The Heavens Never Closed

When Jesus prayed that day at the River Jordan and the heavens opened and the Holy Spirit descended and God the Father spoke in an audible voice, the heavens never closed. The Creator sent His Son, Jesus Christ of Nazareth, on a mission of mercy to the earth to open up the heavens over His creation, mankind. The Creator reopened the heavens over mankind so that the creature (you and I) could have communion with the Creator. <u>The King of Glory perpetually opened the heavens and established the blessings of Psalm 24 for each of us to freely walk in.</u>

Continuing in Genesis 32:2, when Jacob saw the angels, *"he said, 'This is God's camp.' And he called the name of that place Mahanaim."* <u>Mahanaim is a Hebrew word that can mean double camp or double doors, similar to the word we saw in Isaiah 45. In the Hebrew culture a Mahanaim was a place of blessing and a place of communing with Almighty God, Jehovah—the</u>

same One who wants to hold your right hand and the same One that we see in Psalm 24.

A Mahanaim is a place of open heavens, a place where the blessings of Jehovah are released from the heavenly realms to the earthly realms. In these places there is a transfer of heavenly treasure or blessings into the earthly realm and into the lives of God's people or God's friends. This is real; it's a true dynamic in the Kingdom of Heaven. It's an ongoing dynamic today, too. There can be a supernatural exchange between the heavenly realms and the earthly realms. When gates like this are opened, God still pours out His blessings today. Isn't this exciting!

I believe, if you want it, that the Lord is going to allow you to experience a literal Mahanaim. As you learn to discern and to enter into these double gates of breakthrough, there will be a supernatural blessing released from God Almighty into your life. This is the anointing of Psalm 24. I believe you can be delivered. I believe you can be healed. I believe you can be set free. I believe you can have your life transformed. I believe you can be empowered to step into the fullness of your God-ordained destiny. I believe there will be a double door of destiny that will manifest in your life as you read this book. God confirms the Gospel!

Jehovah Will Break in Pieces the Gates of Bronze

Let's go back to Isaiah 45. God goes before us to break open doors and to shatter any locks or hindrances that keep us from walking in the fullness of His destiny for us. We see this in verse 2. God says, "*I will go before you And make the crooked places straight."* This speaks of a transfer of wealth. The Lord will give you the honor and the riches of your enemy.

It gets better: *"I will break in pieces the gates of bronze."* This speaks of shattering the strongholds of the enemy, destroying demonic oppression, destroying sickness, and releasing you from a spirit of poverty and depression or any other thing the enemy has placed upon you through demonic yokes of darkness. God destroys the gates of the enemy!

And Isaiah goes on in 45:2: *"And cut the bars of iron."* What this language means is to utterly destroy the head of the king or utterly destroy the king of the gates of darkness. Remember verse 1 where it says God holds our hands so He will loose the armor or the loins of kings. It is speaking of demonic powers. This passage of scripture speaks of God giving us victory in the spiritual realm that will affect our life and prosperity in the terrestrial, natural, or earthly realm.

It should be noted that the actual original language for the word for *gates* in Isaiah 45:2 could have been more accurately translated as the word *doors.* However, the concept of both gates and doors is still valid and the applications of both words apply to this teaching. Again, sometimes in the Kingdom of Heaven it can be "both/and."

We see this outlined again as we go forward in Isaiah 45:3. The Lord says, *"I will give you the treasures of darkness And hidden riches of secret places. That you may know that I, the LORD, Who call you by your name, Am the God of Israel."* So God gives us revelation of His identity by doing these two things.

This last verse has a pair of meanings, or compound meanings. God can reveal to you and also give to you both the treasures of the heavenly realms and also <u>the hidden spoils or treasures that the enemy has stolen from you and others</u>. These <u>kinds of treasures of darkness are also sequestered in the spiritual realms and can be accessed through spiritual gates as God allows and empowers you</u>.

Jesus is our example of this kind of supernatural ministry. Remember what Jesus said in Revelation 1:18: *"I am He who lives, and was dead, and behold, I am alive forevermore. Amen. And I have the keys of Hades and of Death."* Jesus plundered <u>the treasures of darkness and repossessed the keys</u>! Not only that, but He gives them to His friends! We have learned about this aspect of the ministry of Jesus as <u>He was passing through spiritual gates and going behind the veil outlined previously in Ephesians 4:8-13</u>. I will elaborate on these treasures of darkness and hidden riches of secret places in the next section of this chapter.

The Restoration of Destinies

When Isaiah 45:3 tells us the He will *"give"* us, the Hebrew word translated "give" here is not the regular word for give. It has a profound meaning. It means to give liberally or spectacularly or extravagantly, to set someone in a place of power, to make someone, to refashion a thing, to add to, to appoint, to ascribe, to assign, to avenge or to behead your enemies, to bestow, to bring forth, to charge with favor or to give one prominence, to lift up, to ordain, to pay, to recompense, to render, to restore those things that have been sold or stolen, to send out, to set forth, to send upon a mission, to show secret treasures, to shoot forth or shoot upward or thrust higher, to yield to God, or to yield to the hand of God. Remember, in verse 1 we saw how we can be helped by the hand of God when we learn to submit to the Lord and allow the Lord to hold our hand. This posture is not a posture of meekness, but this type of submission is a posture of spiritual maturity. It is an earmark of becoming mature sons and daughters of God.

We see two types of treasures God wants to give to us as these double gates are opened before us; the key to this is to be in submission to Him. The first is when it says, "*I will give you the treasures of darkness.*" The word translated "treasures" means a depository, an armory, a guarded cellar, a storehouse, or secret treasure or treasure house, just like we saw in verse 2. Today we refer to places such as this as Fort Knox. The United States gold bullion depository is protected and stored at Fort Knox, Kentucky. Even so, there are treasuries and depositories like Fort Knox in the heavenly realms. Jesus said in John 10:10, "*The thief does not come except to steal, and to kill, and to destroy. I have come that they may have life, and that they may have it more abundantly.*"

Where do you think the enemy keeps all those spoils that he has stolen from humanity over the millennia? They are in storehouses of darkness. God wants to burst open the double doors of the storehouses of darkness and restore to His people the treasures, the anointings, the gifts of God, the material wealth that has been stolen from His people. Everything the enemy has stolen from you God promises to restore it to us a hundredfold. Every type of demonic yoke of darkness, like sickness or poverty the enemy has burdened you with, the Lord wants to deliver you and set you totally free. Jesus wants to totally and completely heal us and restore everything that we lost a hundredfold *in this lifetime.*

That has literally happened in my life. Over the years before I knew the Lord as Savior, I lost a lot of things. I lost lands, I lost homes, I lost money, I lost businesses, and I nearly lost my soul. Everything I've lost God has restored to me at least a hundredfold (Mark 10:30). I began to walk this out by unknowingly stepping behind the veil, passing through spiritual gates to enter into the presence and glory of God. When I came back into the earthly realms, God's favor, God's grace was supernaturally attached to me and everything that I touched prospered. I give God glory for that. This is also an example and testimony of the blessing and the double anointing of Psalm 24.

The second type of hidden treasure that God wants to restore to you is the "*hidden riches of secret places.*" This phrase can also have multiple or compound meanings. I personally like this one. It can mean a secret storehouse—hence a secreted, valuable, buried treasure or treasure house. Generally it refers to money or wealth; but it can also mean hidden riches such as silver, gold, and valuable herbs and oils—frankincense and myrrh, for example. It can be hidden treasures or treasures that are not fought for or that one does not labor for to own, possess, or create.

These are wonderful, Godly blessings associated with learning and discerning to see and open spiritual doors into the heavenly realms. The hidden riches of the secret place are Godly treasures. These kinds of Godly treasures can also include the grace, favor, and anointing of God. They can include supernatural revelation and the release or the increase of the gifts of the Holy Spirit into your life. These kinds of Godly treasures can also include a supernatural manifestation and release of material wealth.

The Treasure of the Secret Places

The Book of Proverbs 25:2 says, "*It is the glory of God to conceal a matter, But the glory of kings is to search out a matter.*" You see, God has secrets covered and sequestered in the hidden places. There are restricted rooms in the heavenly realms, and only the friends of the Lord are allowed access to these places. The Lord has hidden secret treasures and unknown mysteries in the Kingdom of God. Revelation 1:5-6 says the blood of Jesus makes us kings and priests. Therefore, you have the liberty to dig these treasures out.

We see a scriptural example of this kind of Kingdom dynamic in Matthew 2:11, speaking of the Magi, the three kings: "*And when they had come into the house, they saw the young Child with Mary His mother, and fell down and worshiped Him. And when they had opened their treasures, they presented gifts to Him: gold, frankincense, and myrrh.*" The King of Glory wants to open up the treasures of heaven and present to you gold, frankincense, and myrrh. Gold speaks of material wealth. In my opinion, frankincense speaks prophetically of the presence of God, the glory of God. Myrrh speaks of healing, miracles, signs, and wonders. These are but a few of the varieties of secret treasures God has in store or in storage for those who love Him.

As good as these heavenly riches may be, these kinds of hidden blessings and anointings get even better. The secret place mentioned in Isaiah 45:3 means concealed riches or treasure, not necessarily money or gold or frankincense or myrrh but spiritual riches—treasure hidden in the heavenly realms or the secret place of the Most High. This is treasure hidden in the secret place—in the presence of God, which we are learning is the habitation of God or the hill of the Lord (Psalm 24). We see this dynamic outlined in Colossians 3:1-2: *"If then you were raised with Christ, seek those things which are above, where Christ is, sitting at the right hand of God. Set your mind on things above, not on things on the earth."*

Let's look at this principle again in Ephesians 1:17: *"May the God of our Lord Jesus Christ, the Father of glory, may give to you the spirit of wisdom and revelation in the knowledge of Him."* These are some of the secret and hidden treasures in the heavenly places. Continuing with verse 18 we read: *"The eyes of your understanding being enlightened,"* which speaks of the seer anointing. And verse 18-19 continues: *"That you may know what is the hope of His calling, what are the riches of the glory of His inheritance in the saints, and what is the exceeding greatness of His power toward us who believe, according to the working of His mighty power"* (*dunamis*, miracle working power, and *kratos*, delegated authority). The ability to see and hear by the Spirit of wisdom and revelation (the seer anointing) are also examples of these kinds of secret treasures and heavenly riches.

Learn to Discern the Heavenly Places

God is giving to His people that *kratos* delegated authority to open up doors to the heavenly realms. That's your inheritance.

Verse 20 tells us about that dunamis power *"which He worked in Christ when He raised Him from the dead and seated Him at His right hand in the heavenly places."* That's our inheritance; we can be seated with Christ in heavenly places. We can pass behind the veil. We can come into the very presence of God. Then we can discern the prayers of Christ, rest in Him, and allow Him to work on our behalf. When this happens, we begin to live our lives in the glory realms. Verse 21 tells us where the heavenly places are located: *"Far above all principality and power and might and dominion, and every name that is named, not only in this age but also in that which is to come."* When we begin to discern and learn how to open up spiritual gates to pass through to rest in the glory of God (go behind the veil), we rise above this earth. We rise above the petty conflicts around us.

This is why Isaiah 26:3 is such an important prophetic promise for the Body of Christ: *"You will keep him in perfect peace, Whose mind is stayed on You, Because he trusts in You."* Paul admonishes in Colossians 3:2 to *"set your mind on things above."* When we can keep our minds, our spirits, our souls, and our bodies focused on Christ and His Kingdom, we rise above the cares of this present age and we begin to live a lifestyle of glory. No matter what's happening around us, we are just walking in the FOG—the favor of God. We are in the glory, and in the glory Christ's Kingdom just comes everywhere we go. The blessings and anointing of Psalm 24 pour out through us and to others in our sphere of influence.

The Hidden Riches of the Secret Places

Really what we are talking about is living our life according to Psalm 91. This is important. The hidden riches of the secret places that we are speaking of found in Isaiah 45 put a whole new implication on Psalm 91. Let's read verses 1 and 2: *"He who dwells in the secret place of the Most High Shall abide under the shadow of the Almighty. I will say of the LORD, "He is my refuge and my fortress."* You see, when we abide in the secret place under the wings of Almighty God, He becomes our fortress. Do you know how many powers or principalities are able to break through the doors of the fortress of God?

The answer to that is zero—none! And when we purpose in our hearts to make the secret place of the Most High our dwelling place, we are protected of God. Going on with the end of verse 2 and verses 3-4, we read, *"My God, in Him I will trust. Surely He shall deliver you from the snare of the fowler And from the perilous pestilence. He shall cover you with His feathers, And under His wings you shall take refuge; His truth shall be your shield and buckler."* Verses 5-7 tell us, *"You shall not be afraid of the terror by night, Nor of the arrow that flies by day, Nor of the pestilence that walks in darkness, Nor of the destruction that lays waste at noonday. A thousand may fall at your side, And ten thousand at your right hand; But it shall not come near you."*

Remember, Jesus gave us the keys to the Kingdom of Heaven. The key to living a Psalm 91 lifestyle is that we must purpose in our hearts to make the secret place of the Most High our dwelling place. Now let's return to the place where we started and conclude the testimony about how the Lord visited me on

February 25, 2014, and released revelation of the blessings of Psalm 24 into my life.

Prayer to Discern the Secret Place

Lord, I ask You, in Jesus' name, to open your good treasure, the heavens, over my life today. Father, I ask that You help me to discern the doors of blessings in my sphere of influence. Remember, Lord, You promised to break in pieces the gates of bronze and to give to me the treasures of darkness and hidden riches of secret places. Lord, I ask for these supernatural blessings to be released into my life now, in Jesus' name. Lord, it is Your pleasure and Your glory to conceal a matter, but it is my supernatural privilege to search out your hidden treasures. Today I make a personal decision to dwell in the secret place of the Most High. I decree that I shall abide under the shadow of the Almighty. I will say that You, O Lord, are my refuge, my strength, and my fortress. I thank You, Lord, for revealing Your secret treasures and pouring Your secrets and blessings out into my life today. In Jesus' name I pray. Amen.

CHAPTER 21

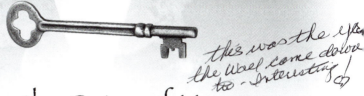

Shaking the Gates of Heaven

this was the yr the wall came down too - Interesting!

(Sent by God) 8 of us sang & spoke over the Golden Gate in Israel Nov. 1989

As we continue to <u>dig out revelation and hidden mysteries</u> from Psalm 24, let's move on and finish looking at verses 7 to 9, where we read, *"And the King of glory shall come in."* Verse 8 expands on that statement: *"Who is this King of glory? The LORD strong and mighty, The LORD mighty in battle."* David then repeats verse 7 in verse 9: *"Lift up your heads, O you gates!"* David is talking about being lifted up or taken away in a supernatural manner to concealed gates or gates to the future. We can enter into the secret place of God's protection.

Remember, to lift up your head means shaking the head, which is the gate (or the captain or ruler of a gate). When the gate shakes, then it opens. When it opens, there is an access to the hill of the Lord and the heavenly dimensions. There we might obtain access to the blessings of the Lord. Here are two important keys to remember as well: praise and worship will help to open up spiritual gates. *We sang these words, too*

Again, I believe that it's possible that these ancient gates and doors that Psalm 24 speaks of are spiritual in nature, perhaps even angelic beings that have the responsibility to open up the dimensions between the earthly realm and the spiritual or the heavenly realms. It's an amazing thing. This puts a whole new paradigm of the concept of "gatekeepers." Perhaps it was a gatekeeper like this that took my hand and directed me as I ascended into the hill of the Lord (heavenly places) while I was in Newfoundland in 2001 and later in Kansas City in 2007?

Apostolic Gatekeepers Will Arise

I believe that this is yet another of the hidden mysteries of the powers of the age to come. God will begin to release the blessings and anointing of Psalm 24 to His people. The Spirit of God is birthing a new type of gatekeeper in the Kingdom of God. These mature sons and daughters of God will be given the grace and authority to co-labor with these Godly angels to open up the spiritual gates into the heavenly dimensions to release the blessings of God into his or her sphere of influence.

Traditionally pastors have been considered gatekeepers of cities and regions. Of course, this will still be an ongoing dynamic of the five-fold ministry. But as the apostolic nature of the church matures and evolves, God will raise up people who will be anointed as spiritual gatekeepers of the Kingdom of Heaven on earth. These apostolic gatekeepers will be given unusual levels of spiritual authority to open and close spiritual gates over cities and even regions. Apostolic gatekeepers will literally be given the keys to the Kingdom of Heaven to open gates of blessing and the Kingdom in their spheres of influence (Matthew 16:19). They, at times, will also be anointed to close gates of darkness in their sphere of influence.

Again, similar to verse 7, the end of verse 9 says, "*Lift up, you everlasting doors! And the King of glory shall come in.*" We are stepping into a day and hour when God is beginning to do some amazing things and He is beginning to release a greater level of trust in His friends. Why? So the King of Glory may come in. How does the King of Glory come in? He comes in through open doors. He comes in from the heavenly dimensions. We need to remember that Jesus is still the One who opens the heavens and Jesus is still the One who empowers His friends to open the heavens by His example.

Verse 10 tells us who He is: "*Who is this King of glory? The Lord of hosts, He is the King of glory.*" The language here means the leader of an organized and skilled troop that is specifically trained for war. In my book *The Sword of the Lord and the Rest of the Lord*, I write about a trance or vision in which I saw the triumphant return of Christ (the King of Glory) and the Lord returning to the earth through such a spiritual gate in the heavenly dimensions with millions and millions of angelic warriors. The Kingdom of God *is* invading the planet earth!

The Bible Was Opened Up

Now back to my story of February 25, 2014, when I had this urge to get into my prayer room. It was my spiritual birthday. It was thirteen years to the day that Jesus came into my heart and saved me and twelve years and nine months to the day that Jesus visited me in Canada. On the 25th day of February 2014, the Spirit kept pressing upon me to get into the prayer room. I was burdened to spend time with the Lord; not to intercede, not to pray. I kept saying, "I've got to get in the prayer room.

I've got to get to my prayer room." Kathy, my wife, was gracious to let me go. We were working at the new King of Glory Ministries International Ministry Apostolic Equipping Center in Moravian Falls, North Carolina. There were lots of tasks that needed to be finished. But I was heavily burdened in the spirit to get in the prayer room.

The second I got in the prayer room and closed the door behind me, the glory of God came down in a great and mighty way. The Lord reminded me of the time He visited me on March 13, 2001, when He spoke to me in what may have been an audible voice out of Psalm 24. He said, "Kevin, I'm going to give you some hidden revelation from Psalm 24." I rested in the glory for hours until the sun set. I felt someone hit the side of the bed.

At that instant I felt my Bible as it seemed to "pop" open and thumped against my right side. I continue resting in the glory as I reach over to feel for my Bible (now open) beside me on the bed. It certainly was closed before. I put my hand on it and started weeping because I knew it had opened to Psalm 24. I rested there in the glory for another hour or so. When I finally turned the light on, guess where the Bible had opened up to? Psalm 24.

I asked the Lord, "Lord, what's going on?" He said, "Remember how your old King James Bible opened up to Acts chapter 1 in Daisy's cabin?" I said, "Yes, Lord; I remember!" He said, "Well, I just sent that same angel back to minister for you by giving you more revelation."

I believe God is releasing hidden revelation like this not only from Psalm 24 but from many places in the Bible. I believe that there is a supernatural grace and a supernatural opening to step into these dimensions in this day. This is not because of who *we are* but because of who *He is*. I believe that the time is growing short and the return of Christ is at hand. God wants to raise up men and women from two to a hundred and two who will be able to see and hear those things God has prepared for us because we love Him. That's the key right there: if we love God, He will show us these hidden and mysterious things.

This is the apostolic love of Christ, and I believe that anybody can step into this dynamic of Christ's Kingdom freely. I write about the apostolic love of Christ in the book *Unlocking The Hidden Mysteries of the Powers of the Age to Come*. It's not about being a super star; it's not about being an apostle or prophet or pastor or teacher or evangelist. Anyone can step into this aspect of the seer realms. Yes, God does have chosen vessels, because the scripture says that; but I believe God has chosen you. I believe the New Testament where it tells us "*whosoever*," (See King James Version Mark 8:34; John 11:26; Romans 10:11, 13; Acts 10:43; 1 John 4:15.) Yes, scripture teaches that Paul was a chosen vessel (Acts 9:15) but it always says "whosoever" too. The promises of God are always to whosoever in the New Testament.

So let's return to Isaiah 45, beginning with verse 4: "*For Jacob My servant's sake.*" Remember, Jacob received the blessings of God at the Mahanaim that we read about in Genesis 32. Continuing with Isaiah 45:4, we read, "*And Israel My elect, I have even called you by your name; I have named you, though you have not known Me.*" This is another Hebraism. The Hebrew word used here is *yada*, which means to know; or to see; or to experience in a tangible way, to feel, taste, smell, or touch. It means to discover a friend; to discover a kinsman redeemer; to be allowed to know; to be given knowledge; or to have revelation of God or Jehovah.

The NIV version of this passage of scripture says, "*I summon you by name and bestow on you a title of honor, though you do not acknowledge me.*" We could just say that it is to have the understanding that we can become the friend of God; that we can pass behind the veil and come into the glory to experience the realms of heaven, the glory of God. You see, no longer is heaven "way up there." Heaven is all around us. We *can* experience it. Praise God! There is an acceleration of this type of grace and this type of supernatural outpouring at this season. I believe that many of you will have a supernatural encounter with Jehovah as you pray the prayer to activate and release the blessings of Psalm 24 into your lives. There is a grace being given by God to His friends to know Him. We can pass through the double doors of blessing.

Put Me in Remembrance

There is a wonderful passage of scripture that I like to remember when I come into the very presence of God. It is in Isaiah 43:26. The Lord speaking says, "*Put Me in remembrance; Let us contend together; State your case, that you may be acquitted.*" That is what we experience when we enter into the presence of God and we state our case and remind God that He is a God of mercy; He is a God of grace.

Back to Isaiah 45:5: "*I am the Lord, and there is no other; There is no God besides Me. I will gird you.*" That means He will strengthen you, empower you, and give you everything you need to fulfill your destiny. Continuing with verse 5 we read: *"Though you have not known Me." Verses 6-7* tell us why the Lord does these things: *"That they may know from the rising of the sun to its setting That there is none besides Me. I am the Lord, and there is no other; I form the light and create darkness, I make peace and create calamity; I, the Lord, do all these things."* The Lord goes on in verse 8: *"Rain down, you heavens, from above, And let the skies pour down righteousness; Let the earth open, let them bring forth salvation, And let righteousness spring up together. I, the Lord, have created it."*

I believe there is an impartation that God wants me to release to you. I believe God wants me to bless you and to release an activation, an impartation, and a supernatural blessing into your life. If you have a need for a miracle or healing, you can also receive your healing as you read the prayer below. I want to decree these blessings over you. I want to pray for the blessings of Psalm 24 to be poured out into your life. I want you to put your hand on your heart and receive as you read this prophetic declaration and prayer.

Prayer of Prophetic Declarations and Miracles and Healing

Lord, I thank You for the ministry of Jesus. I thank You, Father God, that Jesus came and shed His blood to make us righteous and holy, to make us kings and priests before our God and our Father. I thank You, Father God, that the whole family in Heaven and in earth is named by You;

that we were knit together, Father, in our mother's womb by Your hand; and that You have a supernatural destiny on each of us. Father, I decree that it's the love of God that unlocks the hidden mysteries of Your Kingdom.

Lord, I decree that we have stepped into a day and a time when our eyes will see and our ears will hear and we will discern those things that You have prepared for those who love You. And, Lord, right now we say that we do love You. Lord, I ask that You would grant to us according to the riches of Your glory that we would be strengthened with might and power through the Holy Spirit in our inner man, in our spirit.

And, Father, <u>I'm asking now in the name of Jesus Christ that the Lord would dwell in our hearts through faith, that we would be rooted and grounded in the love of God; so that we might comprehend with all the saints what is the width and length and depth and height that we might personally know the love of God, that passes our ability to comprehend. Lord, I ask now that we would be filled with all the fullness of God. And, Lord, we ask You—</u> who is able to do exceedingly abundantly above all that we could think, ask, or imagine, according to the power that works within us—that You would release Your good gifts to Your friends now. And to You, Lord, be the power and the glory and the honor forever and ever, in Jesus' mighty name.

Keep your hand on your chest.

Father, I decree and release the blessings of Psalm 24 right now over those reading this book. Who shall receive the blessing of the Lord? Those who have clean hands and a pure heart; they shall receive the blessing of the Lord. Father, now I decree blessing. Father, I thank You that You will bless those who bless us and You will bless those who curse us. Father, I ask that You would release the blessing of Jehovah; I ask that You would release the righteousness from the God of our salvation. Let it come, God. Let Your blessings rain down upon us now, Lord; let Your blessings rain down from the heavenly realms. Father, we speak to the heavens in the name of Jesus. We say thank You, Lord, that You're opening up the heavens even now.

We say, "Heavens open, in the name of the Lord." The heavens are opening over your life and God beginning to release His blessings in tangible ways to you. Finances are turning around—blessings coming in a tangible way in terms of finances, money coming from unexpected places. I decree the blessing of Psalm 24 is released in Jesus' name.

Father, we thank You that You are releasing healing for our eyes and our ears right now, in the name of the Lord.

Someone reading this is struggling with a potentially life-threatening sickness or disease.

Lord, we thank You that You are allowing us to ascend to the hill of the Lord right now. We thank You that in the heavenly realms there is no sickness, there is no disease, there is no leukemia, there is no blood disease or any other sickness. Father, we take authority over every blood condition and sickness right now, in Jesus' name.

Diabetes be healed, in the name of the Lord.

Father, we take authority over sickness associated with colds and flu.

If you are suffering with that, it is going to lift off. As you rise up tomorrow, your cough will clear, your congestion in your lungs will go, in Jesus' name. We take authority over the spirit of cold and influenza right now, in the name of Jesus!

Father, we say that Your angels are welcome to descend into the lives of those reading this right now. Let Your angels of healing come, Lord. Thank You for the angels of miracles and healing that You are releasing into people's lives right now, Lord. We welcome them now, in Jesus' name.

Someone is being healed of chronic migraine headaches, specifically behind your eyes. Migraine headaches are being healed! Hallelujah!

Lord, thank You for healing chronic migraine headaches right now.

Angels are coming down and doing surgery in hearts. Angelic beings are touching hearts. Ventricles and aortas are being replaced. Heart congestion and angina be healed right now, In Jesus' name. Hearts are being healed, not just physically sick hearts but hearts that have been broken.

Father, thank You for releasing angels of new days. Thank You for new days and new ways.

The winter is going to pass and new days are coming.

Father, we just release the blessings of Your Kingdom right now, in Jesus' mighty name.

Generational conditions of chronic pain in the body are breaking off right now, in Jesus' name. A generational curse of arthritis is being broken, in the name of the Lord. We take authority over this thing called arthritis and command it to go, in Jesus' name.

Knees are being healed, in Jesus' name. Angels of creative miracles are touching knees. Some who have had ligaments and tendons damaged will feel movement in your knee, where tendons and ligaments are being recreated, in the name of the Lord. Creative miracles are happening right NOW!

We command every kind of cysts, growths, or tumors to dissolve, in Jesus' name. Cysts, growths, and tumors are dissolving and going away. Check them and see if they are gone.

In the name of Jesus Christ of Nazareth, Father, we thank You that the heavens are coming down and that we are receiving every spiritual blessing in heavenly places, including healing and miracles. Father, we ask You to release those angels of healings and miracles to those reading this book. NOW!

We thank You, Father, for angels of dentistry. Father, we thank You for new enamel and amalgam and fillings being transformed into silver and gold. Father, we thank You for releasing Your angels of dentistry to come to touch these readers, in Jesus' name.

If you need a dental miracle, check. Please take time to check your teeth in the mirror! Maybe the Lord gave new enamel and your amalgam fillings are gone! Maybe the Lord turned your amalgam into gold, or maybe He just gave you a new golden crown! Just put this book down and go look in the mirror! Look at least seven times! Keep on seeking, keep on asking, keep on looking, and check for your dental miracle! New teeth are being created now! Dental miracles come forth NOW! Amen!

Back and neck pain is being healed.

Deaf ears are being healed. For someone it seems like the volume of your hearing is being turned up and your ears are being healed, right now! Deafness is healed in the name of Jesus! Deaf ears are popping open even NOW!

Angels are coming with eye salve.

Father, we welcome Your angels that are anointing eyes to see and anointing ears to hear.

Acceleration in dreams, trances, and visions is coming. God is visiting many in dreams starting even tonight. It may be a reactivation of a dormant gift of dreams. A sweet presence of the Lord is coming.

Father, we thank You for the peace and holiness of God that comes down and rests upon the readers even now. Let Your peace come down, O God, Jehovah. Give us eyes to see and ears to hear. Father, release the blessings now. Thank You, Father, for pouring out the impartation and activation of the seer realms and the blessings of Psalm

24 that are coming upon those reading these words right now. In Jesus' name! Amen! Hallelujah!

Epilogue

We have entered into a new season. We have crossed over a God-ordained, *kiaros* moment of time. The Lord, Elohim, the Creator of the heavens and the earth, is opening up the gates and doors of heaven to His friends. The Father is giving free access for you to "come up here" into the heavenly realms to "see what must take place after this."

The blessings of Psalm 24 have been accelerated and are manifesting in many people's lives around the earth at this day and hour. The anointings and the blessings of Psalm 24 can activate and be poured out into your life as well today. Just purpose in your heart to believe to receive. Learn to discern the Gospel or the Truth.

You *can* ascend into the hill of the Lord. You *can* stand in His holy place today, because the blood of Jesus Christ of Nazareth can wash you and cleanse you. The blood of Jesus is the most powerful substance in the universe. The blood of Jesus can give you clean hands. The Lord Jesus can recreate in you a pure heart. The blood of Jesus can purge us with hyssop, and we shall be clean. The Lord can wash us, and we shall be recreated whiter than snow. The Messiah, the Savior, can forgive your sins and transform your life.

The blood of Jesus enables you to receive blessing from the Lord and the righteousness from the God of your salvation. You can ascend into the hill of the Lord and go boldly where few men have gone before. You can enter into the most holy place behind the veil, just as Jesus our Forerunner did. There you can learn to discern the prayers and activities of the Messiah. There you can be empowered to discern spiritual gates and position yourself to receive the blessings and anointings of the Lord found in Psalm 24. King David brilliantly prophesied of a day that was to come when God's friends would be empowered to seek His face and to literally ascend into the mountain or habitation of the Lord God Almighty, Elohim! That day, that supernatural moment of time, is now.

The Lord is raising up mature sons and daughters of God who will be like Christ. They will learn to see into and to hear clearly from the heavenly realms. They will see and hear what their heavenly Father is doing; and then, like Jesus, they will simply do those things and amazing manifestations of the Kingdom of Heaven will transpire.

We can position ourselves to receive the blessings of Almighty God in the glory realms. God is still opening up to His friends His good treasure, the heavens, and raining out supernatural blessings today (Deuteronomy 28:12) Just believe for the Spirit of the Lord to release an impartation of the seer anointing into your life as you have read this book. As you pray the prayers in the Table of Prayers consistently, believe for an activation of the seer anointing to be released in your life by the Spirit of the living God for such a time as this. Keep praying the prayers of activation on the Table of Prayers until you receive your breakthrough and the doors and windows of heaven open over your life.

Lift up your heads, shake the gates of heaven and decree: King of Glory—Come! Lord Jesus, help us to see things in a new way. Help us to hear things in a new way. Open up Your everlasting doors and let the heavens be opened over my life now!

Prayer for Eyes to See and Ears to Hear

Father, thank You for sending Jesus, the King of Glory. Thank You, Father, that through the shed blood of Jesus Christ and through the finished work of the Cross of Calvary, You have made us kings and priests who can come boldly before the throne of grace. Thank You, Father God, that the blood of Jesus make us righteous and Holy to minister to our God and Father. Lord, as I share Your Word, I ask You that it would go forward in power and that it would not return void—that it would pierce the hearts of those who read it.

Lord, I ask that as I share the Gospel and the testimonies that You have placed upon my heart, that there would be an activation and impartation of the seer realm which would come upon people's lives and that they would have ears to hear and eyes to see—that our eyes would see and our ears would hear things that we would not have imagined possible. Father, I thank You that we have stepped into a new dispensation of time, that You are doing amazing things in the earthly realms. Father, I thank You that the Kingdom of Heaven is truly invading our sphere of influence. Thank you Lord, for opening the heavens over my life now. And we promise to give You the praise and all of the honor and the glory for everything that You've done and everything that You are going to do; in Jesus mighty name, Amen. Hallelujah!

Psalm 24

The earth is the Lord's, and all its fullness, The world and those who dwell therein. For He has founded it upon the seas, And established it upon the waters. Who may ascend into the hill of the Lord? Or who may stand in His holy place? He who has clean hands and a pure heart, Who has not lifted up his soul to an idol, Nor sworn deceitfully. He shall receive blessing from the Lord, and righteousness from the God of his salvation. This is Jacob, the generation of those who seek Him, Who seek Your face. Selah Lift up your heads, O you gates! And be lifted up, you everlasting doors! And the King of glory shall come in. Who is this King of glory? The Lord strong and mighty, The Lord mighty in battle. Lift up your heads, O you gates! Lift up, you everlasting doors! And the King of glory shall come in. Who is this King of glory? The Lord of hosts, He is the King of glory. Selah

Table of Prayers

Prayer of Reception

Lord, I choose to believe to receive. Father, in Jesus' name, I purpose in my heart to believe to receive the prophetic promises that the Holy Spirit has placed into these pages. Lord, I am ready, I am willing, and I choose to receive everything that You are seeking to release to me from the Kingdom of Heaven though this book. Holy Spirit, I ask that You would guide me and teach me. Lord, I ask that You would open my spiritual eyes and activate my spiritual ears to see and hear in a Christ like way. Lord Jesus, You said that to me it has been given and granted to know the hidden mysteries of the Kingdom of Heaven. Today, Lord, I choose to revive those blessings and revelations that You have hidden for me in the Holy Scriptures. Help me to see the keys to unlock the hidden mysteries of Your word and of Your Kingdom to me now. Lord, let Your Kingdom come into my life on earth as it is in heaven today. In the name of Jesus Christ of Nazareth I Pray. Amen!

Prayer to Activate Godly Discernment

Lord, I ask You to reveal to me the secrets and hidden mysteries that eye has not seen nor ear heard. Lord, I ask You to ignite my heart by Your Spirit and let the Kingdom of heaven enter into my heart. Reveal to me the mysteries and the secret things that You have prepared for those who love You. I ask You, Father, in the name of Jesus, to reveal the fellowship of the mysteries and the unsearchable riches found in Christ to me. Reveal them to my spirit. O Lord, open my eyes to see the mysteries hidden in the Kingdom of Heaven. Lord, help me to discern the manifold wisdom of God. Lord I am asking You to give me eyes to see and ears to hear in a new and supernatural way. In the name of Jesus I pray. Amen!

Prayer of Freedom

Father, in the name of Jesus I choose to believe this testimony. Lord, the Bible tells us that You are no respecter of persons. What You did in Kevin's life You can do in my life. Lord, I confess that I am struggling with sin and addiction. I repent now and ask the Lord Jesus Christ to become the Lord of my life. Jesus, I ask that You would save me now and set me free from this addiction. Lord, deliver me from every demonic power and every generational curse associated with this addiction now. In Jesus' name, I command every demon of addiction to loose your assignment against my life right now. Addiction, go, in Jesus' name! Lord, I thank You for saving me and setting me free now. I choose to walk in the paths that You have chosen for me, Lord. And I choose to serve You and only You, Lord, all the days of my life. And Lord, I thank You for making me into a new creation with a new God-ordained destiny. Help me, Lord, to see and hear clearly from You today and every day. Amen.

A Prayer Modeled After Jabez

O Lord, I ask that You would bless me indeed. Lord, I am asking that You would expand my territory and allow me to hear and to see in new and heavenly ways. O Lord, that You would place Your mighty right hand upon me and strengthen me to walk in the paths that You have preordained for me to walk in. O Lord, that You would bless me in a great and mighty way. And Father, I ask in Jesus' name that I might not be the cause of any pain. In the mighty name of Jesus I pray. Amen.

Prayer of Transformation

Lord, Your word teaches that if anyone is Christ he becomes a new creation. Lord, I choose to commit my ways to You right now. I choose to be in Christ. And Father, I am asking You to release and activate a supernatural transformation in my life and circumstances. Lord, take me from the darkness and translate me into the Kingdom of Your Son and into Your Kingdom of Light. Ignite a supernatural transformation in my life and set a heavenly fire deep down in my soul. Transform me into the very image of your beloved Son, Jesus. Lord, help me to see the reality of Your Kingdom and step into the fullness of the destiny that You have prepared for me. In Jesus' name I pray. Amen!

Prayer for Geographical Obedience

Father, by You all things both in heaven and upon earth were created. Lord, You created time. And at this time, Father, I ask You, in the might Name of Jesus Christ of Nazareth, to give me favor with time. Lord, I ask that I would discern the times and seasons in my life. Help me to have supernatural revelation each day of Your perfect timing in my life. Help me to be geographically and chronologically obedient to Your Spirit. Lord, give me revelation and show me where I should be and when I should be there. Help me to know, without doubt or shadow of wavering, what is Your good, acceptable, and the perfect will for my life. And Lord, help me to walk in Your perfect timing in all things. Father, You give wisdom to the wise and knowledge to those who have understanding; and I ask You, O Lord, to bless me with understanding of the times and seasons of heaven for my life right now. In Jesus name I pray. Amen.

just a note

Kim   Paul Keith

Dear
Blessings
I am praying that no weapon formed
against Kim & his family, team
& ministry can ~~ever~~ penetrate
the Blood of Jesus in any ~~way~~
way! We ask for a 100 fold
blessings of healings, peace, joy
love & prosperity for the whole
family. I ~~cover them~~ Surround them with
fire walls of protection — discerned
about all their property & their
travels. Those as fire angels
of protection. Every part of
their bodies

special

Dangerous Prayer

Lord, if You are real, then I want to see You. I want to experience Your love and glory first hand. Lord, I want to be like that guy called Saul in Acts 9. Yes, Lord! Let a light from heaven shine upon me! Jesus, come and speak to me Face-to-face, like a man does to a friend. Jesus, if You are real, then I want You to come and visit me. I want to be knocked off of my horse. I want you to appear to me like You appeared to that dude Saul. Show me a light from heaven! Reveal Yourself to me, Jesus. Let me be knocked off of my high horse! Let me have to get up from the road picking gravel from between my teeth. Lord, anoint and empower some guy like Ananias to come and lay his hands upon me that I might may receive my sight and have my spiritual vision activated! O Lord, that I might be filled with the fullness of Your Holy Spirit. Open my eyes to see You, Lord Jesus. Open my ears to hear You speak to me, my God! Help me to see and hear in a new and supernatural way. In Jesus name I pray. Amen!

Prayer to See and Hear in a New Way

Father, Your word says that the testimony of Jesus is the spirit of prophesy. So, Lord, according to the last testimony, I ask You now to begin to help me to see in a new way. Lord, in the name of Jesus Christ, I ask You, Father, that I would begin to hear in a new way. Holy Spirit, I ask for You to guide and to teach me today. Holy

Ghost, help me to learn to see and to hear in a new way. Lord, help to reveal to my spirit what Jesus desired for me to understand when He taught in Luke 8:18: "Take heed how you hear. For whoever has, to him more will be given." Lord, I am asking that more will be given to me to help me to hear the way that You wish for me to hear of God. And right now I thank You, Lord, for opening up my spiritual ears to hear and opening up my spiritual eyes to see in new and amazing ways. In Jesus' name I pray. Amen!

Prayer for Boldness to See and Hear in a New Way

Father, in Jesus' name I ask that You grant to Your servant boldness to see and hear the way that You want me to see and hear. It is right in Your sight, O God, to listen and to hear You more clearly rather than listen to the doctrine of man. Lord, I ask that You open up the seer realms to me so that I am empowered by Your Spirit to see and hear clearly from Your Kingdom. Then I shall decree: "For I cannot but speak the things which I have seen and heard." In Jesus' name, I pray. Amen.

Prayer for Manifestations of the Kingdom

Lord, I thank You that Your Kingdom is a supernatural place. Today I choose to recognize that You created the heavens and the earth. The earth is Yours, Lord, and it is a supernatural place. Today, Lord, I ask You in the mighty Name of Jesus to help me to discern and perceive the supernatural aspects of the terrestrial or earthly realms. Give me eyes to see and discern the places and times where You open the heavens over my life. In Jesus' name I pray. Amen.

Prayer for the Cleansing of the Heart (Based on Psalm 51)

Father, today in the mighty name of Jesus Christ of Nazareth, I ask You, Lord, that You would search my heart. Lord, search my inner parts; and through the power and ministry of the precious Holy Spirit, I ask that You would reveal anything that is hidden in the chambers of my heart. Lord, shine the light of Your Kingdom upon me and uncover any hidden agendas or hidden sins that I am not aware of. Lord, reveal any idols that I have unwittingly allowed to reign in my heart. Lord, I ask that You would heal and deliver me right now, in the name of Jesus Christ. Lord, I pray that You would minister to me according to the precepts of Psalm 51. Lord Jesus, wash me thoroughly from my iniquity and cleanse me from my sin. I acknowledge my transgressions, and my sin is always before me. Against You, You only, O Lord, have I sinned, and done evil in Your sight. Lord, may You be found just when You speak and blameless when You judge me, O God.

You are a merciful God. Remember, O Lord, that I was brought forth in iniquity and in sin my mother conceived me. Reveal Your truth and Your nature in my inward parts, and in the hidden parts may You allow me to know wisdom. Purge me with hyssop, and I shall be clean. Wash me with the blood of Jesus and I shall be whiter than snow. Make me hear with joy and gladness that even my bones may rejoice in You alone, Lord. Hide Your face from my sins, and blot out all my iniquities. And I pray in the name of Jesus that You would create in me a clean heart, O God, and renew a steadfast spirit within me. Cast me not away from Your presence, and do not take Your Holy Spirit from me. Lord, I ask that You restore to me the fullness of the joy of Your salvation, and uplift and heal me by the power of Your generous Spirit. Amen!

Prayer of the Father's Blessing

Father, You promised to bless us with every blessing in the heavenly places. And today, heavenly Father, I ask that You would pour out upon me a Father's blessing. Father, in Jesus' name I pray that You would open the windows of heaven and release Your good treasure to me. Pour out Your grace and favor upon my life. It is Your good pleasure to give me the Kingdom; and today, Lord, I am asking that the Kingdom of Heaven would come upon my life in a fresh and new way. O Father, I ask that you would bless me indeed! Amen.

Table of Prayers

Prayer of Covering

Lord Jesus, thank You for Your blood. I cover myself in Your blood right now, and I thank You that Your blood is the most powerful substance upon the earth. Thank You, Lord, for washing me and totally forgiving me from by sins with Your own blood. Lord Jesus, today I recognize that by the power of Your blood, I have been transformed into a king and royal priest. And I thank You, Lord, that these privileges open up the doors and gates of the heavenly realms and make a way for me to minister to my God and Father. Thank You, Lord Jesus, because You have redeemed us to God by Your blood. Thank You, Lord, that I may ascend into the hill of the Lord. As I mature and learn to walk in greater levels holiness and purity each day, I ask that You would give me further revelation of what it means to bind on earth and that I might also learn how to loose Your Kingdom upon the earth and understand the mysteries of what will be loosed in heaven. In Jesus' name I pray. Amen.

Prayer for Discernment of Spiritual Gates

Lord, I ask, in the mighty name of Jesus Christ, for You to open my spiritual eyes. Lord, help me to discern the prayers of Jesus. Father, I ask that You would give me the grace to discern the spiritual gates that You have ordained for me to perceive. Help me to ascend unto the hill of the Lord. Lord, help me to position myself correctly at Your spiritual gates to release breakthroughs from the heavenly realms into my life in the natural realm. Lord, help me to access the blessings of Jehovah from Your word in my life today. Lord, I ask in Jesus' name that You would activate the double anointing and the blessings of Psalm 24 in my life. Lord Jesus, release the revelation and the keys into my life to open and close the spiritual gates around me. And, Lord, I ask for wisdom and revelation of the times and season to do these things. In Jesus' name I pray. Amen.

Prayer to Possess the Gates of Your Enemies

Lord, I ask in the name of Jesus that You help me to understand the hidden mysteries of spiritual gates. Jesus, I ask that You give me eyes to see and a spirit to discern in a new way. Help me to recognize these spiritual principles and understand how to receive from the open heaven of Your Kingdom. Lord, also give me the wisdom and authority to close the doors of the enemy that open and are affecting my life. Lord, help me to discern and to possess the gates of my enemies. In Jesus' name I pray. Amen.

Prayer to Be Truly Blessed and Highly Favored

Lord, I thank You that I am truly blessed and highly favored with great, great grace and divine intervention in my life today. I am a King's kid and a royal priest *according to the order of Melchizedek, and I am walking in the FOG—the favor of God! Amen.*

Prayer to Discern the Secret Place

Lord, I ask You, in Jesus' name, to open your good treasure, the heavens, over my life today. Father, I ask that You help me to discern the doors of blessings in my sphere of influence. Remember, Lord, You promised to break in pieces the gates of bronze and to give to me the treasures of darkness and hidden riches of secret places. Lord, I ask for these supernatural blessings to be released into my life now, in Jesus' name. Lord, it is Your pleasure and Your glory to conceal a matter, but it is my supernatural privilege to search out your hidden treasures. Today I make a personal decision to dwell in the secret place of the Most High. I decree that I shall abide under the shadow of the Almighty. I will say that You, O Lord, are my refuge, my strength, and my fortress. I thank You, Lord, for revealing Your secret treasures and pouring Your secrets and blessings out into my life today. In Jesus' name I pray. Amen.

Prayer of Prophetic Declarations and Miracles and Healing

Lord, I thank You for the ministry of Jesus. I thank You, Father God, that Jesus came and shed His blood to make us righteous and holy, to make us kings and priests before our God and our Father. I thank You, Father God, that the whole family in Heaven and in earth is named by You; that we were knit together, Father, in our mother's womb by Your hand; and that You have a supernatural destiny on each of us. Father, I decree that it's the love of God that unlocks the hidden mysteries of Your Kingdom.

Lord, I decree that we have stepped into a day and a time when our eyes will see and our ears will hear and we will discern those things that You have prepared for those who love You. And, Lord, right now we say that we do love You. Lord, I ask that You would grant to us according to the riches of Your glory that we would be strengthened with might and power through the Holy Spirit in our inner man, in our spirit.

And, Father, I'm asking now in the name of Jesus Christ that the Lord would dwell in our hearts through faith, that we would be rooted and grounded in the love of God; so that we might comprehend with all the saints what is the width and length and depth and height that we might personally know the love of God, that passes our ability to comprehend. Lord, I ask now that we would be filled with all the fullness of God. And, Lord, we ask You— who is able to do exceedingly abundantly above all that we could think, ask, or imagine, according to the power that works within us—that You would release Your good gifts to Your friends now. And to You, Lord, be the power and the glory and the honor forever and ever, in Jesus' mighty name.

Keep your hand on your chest.

Father, I decree and release the blessings of Psalm 24 right now over those reading this book. Who shall receive the blessing of the Lord? Those who have clean hands and a pure heart; they shall receive the blessing of the Lord. Father, now I decree blessing. Father, I thank You that You will bless those who bless us and You will curse those who curse us. Father, I ask that You would release the blessing of Jehovah; I ask that You would release the righteousness from the God of our salvation. Let it come, God. Let Your blessings rain down upon us now, Lord; let Your blessings rain down from the heavenly realms. Father, we speak to the heavens in the name of Jesus. We say thank You, Lord, that You're opening up the heavens even now.

We say, "Heavens open, in the name of the Lord." The heavens are opening over your life and God beginning to release His blessings in tangible ways to you. Finances are turning around—blessings coming in a tangible way in terms of finances, money coming from unexpected places. I decree the blessing of Psalm 24 is released in Jesus' name.

Father, we thank You that You are releasing healing for our eyes and our ears right now, in the name of the Lord.

Someone reading this is struggling with a potentially life-threatening sickness or disease.

Lord, we thank You that You are allowing us to ascend to the hill of the Lord right now. We thank You that in the heavenly realms there is no sickness, there is no disease, there is no leukemia, there is no blood disease or any other sickness. Father, we take authority over every blood condition and sickness right now, in Jesus' name.

Diabetes be healed, in the name of the Lord.

Father, we take authority over sickness associated with colds and flu.

If you are suffering with that, it is going to lift off. As you rise up tomorrow, your cough will clear; your congestion in your lungs will go, in Jesus' name. We take authority over the spirit of cold and influenza right now, in the name of Jesus!

Father, we say that Your angels are welcome to descend into the lives of those reading this right now. Let Your angels of healing come, Lord. Thank You for the angels of miracles and healing that You are releasing into people's lives right now, Lord. We welcome them now, in Jesus' name.

Someone is being healed of chronic migraine headaches, specifically behind your eyes. Migraine headaches are being healed! Hallelujah!

Lord, thank You for healing chronic migraine headaches right now.

Angels are coming down and doing surgery in hearts. Angelic beings are touching hearts. Ventricles and aortas are being replaced. Heart congestion and angina be healed right now, In Jesus' name. Hearts are being healed, not just physically sick hearts but hearts that have been broken.

Father, thank You for releasing angels of new days. Thank You for new days and new ways.

The winter is going to pass and new days are coming.

Father, we just release the blessings of Your Kingdom right now, in Jesus' mighty name.

Generational conditions of chronic pain in the body are breaking off right now, in Jesus' name. A generational curse of arthritis is being broken, in the name of the

Lord. We take authority over this thing called arthritis and command it to go, in Jesus' name.

Knees are being healed, in Jesus' name. Angels of creative miracles are touching knees. Some who have had ligaments and tendons damaged will feel movement in your knee, where tendons and ligaments are being recreated, in the name of the Lord. Creative miracles are happening right NOW!

We command any kinds of cysts, growths, or tumors to dissolve, in Jesus' name. Cysts, growths, and tumors are dissolving and going away. Check them and see if they are gone.

In the name of Jesus Christ of Nazareth, Father, we thank You that the heavens are coming down and that we are receiving every spiritual blessing in heavenly places, including healing and miracles. Father, we ask You to release those angels of healings and miracles to those reading this book. NOW!

We thank You, Father, for angels of dentistry. Father, we thank You for new enamel and amalgam and fillings being transformed into silver and gold. Father, we thank You for releasing Your angels of dentistry to come to touch these readers, in Jesus' name.

Table of Prayers

If you need a dental miracle, check. Please take time to check your teeth in the mirror! Maybe the Lord gave new enamel and your amalgam fillings are gone! Maybe the Lord turned your amalgam into gold, or maybe He just gave you a new golden crown! Just put this book down and go look in the mirror! Look at least seven times! Keep on seeking, keep on asking, keep on looking, and check for your dental miracle! New teeth are being created now! Dental miracles come forth NOW! Amen!

Back and neck pain is being healed.

Deaf ears are being healed. For someone it seems like the volume of your hearing is being turned up and your ears are being healed, right now! Deafness is healed in the name of Jesus! Deaf ears are popping open even NOW!

Angels are coming with eye salve.

Father, we welcome Your angels that are anointing eyes to see and anointing ears to hear.

Acceleration in dreams, trances, and visions is coming. God is visiting many in dreams starting even tonight. It may be a reactivation of a dormant gift of dreams. A sweet presence of the Lord is coming.

Father, we thank You for the peace and holiness of God that comes down and rests upon the readers even now.

Let Your peace come down, O God, Jehovah. Give us eyes to see and ears to hear. Father, release the blessings now. Thank You, Father, for pouring out the impartation and activation of the seer realms and the blessings of Psalm 24 that are coming upon those reading these words right now. In Jesus' name! Amen! Hallelujah!

Prayers of Activation, Impartation, and Declarations of Glory

Father, today I decree that the heavens are opening and that I will make the secret place of the Most High my dwelling place. I shall abide under the shadow of the Almighty. Amen.

We give You the glory, O Lord. Father, we thank You that You are opening up the windows and doors of heaven today. We give You the glory, O Lord. We give You the glory, O Lord.

I see the windows of heaven opening, and I see God raining down blessings. You may actually feel the raindrops falling upon you—raindrops of blessings coming down from the heavenlies, showers of blessings falling down from the secret place.

Lord, we thank You that You are opening up Your good treasures today; opening up the heavens, raining down the treasures of the heavenlies. Let Your Kingdom come, O Lord. Let Your will be done, O Lord, in our lives here on earth as it is in the heavenlies.

I see doors opening over lives right now. Blessings are raining down—grace and favor from God Almighty coming down. The Lord says, "Just take My hand. Just take My hand and walk with Me. Let My Word be a light unto your path. Rest in the secret place. Come under the shadow of My wings right now. Just choose to rest in Me."

Do you smell the rain? There are thunders and lightnings from the heavenlies. God is saying yes and amen right now. *Let it be so, Lord.* There's a rain coming down; there's a rain coming down; there's a heavy rain falling down from the heavenlies. There are showers of blessings falling, showers of healing.

Lord, we receive it today! We receive the showers of Your love, showers of Your grace and mercy.

The Lord is opening up eyes to see and ears to hear right now. I see angels descending riding on the winds of heaven, angels descending into the place that you are in right now. Wherever you are reading this book, angels are coming down with eye salve to anoint your eyes. Angels are coming down with cornucopia or shofars. God is putting horns in your ears to hear. You are going to begin to see in a new way. You are going to begin to hear in a new way.

"Come up here," says the Lord. "Come up here," says the Lord. "Come up here," says the Lord. "Come up here," says the Lord. "Come up here," says the Lord."Come up here," says the

Prayers of Activation, Impartation, and Declarations of Glory

Lord. "Come up here," says the Lord. "I will show you things, hidden and mysterious thing. I will give unto thee the secret things, hidden treasures and mysteries of the secret places."

There is a steady rain falling now. He's raining down His love. He's raining down His grace. Lord, we receive it today. It's getting heavy; it's getting heavy. Thank You, Lord. The Kingdom is coming down now!

Thus saith the Lord; thus saith God Almighty, "This day I choose to open up the heavens in your life. This day I open up the heavens within your heart. Just call upon Me anytime. Call upon Me anytime and you can come up here into the secret place and dwell with Me. Come up here and dwell with Me," says the Lord. "Come up here into the heavenlies."

Open wide ye gates; open wide ye gates.

King of Glory, come in to our heart right now. King of Glory, You're welcome here. King of Glory, we adore You. We worship You today, O God. Give us rain in this heavenly place. Let the rain fall upon us now. Let Your people get soaking wet with the heavenly realms. Let it come down. Let Your Kingdom come down, O Lord, on earth as it is in heaven.

"And from the throne proceeded lightnings, thunderings" (Revelation 4:5).

Let the rain fall down, O God. Let the rain come down here. Thank You, Lord, for opening up the windows of heavens in our lives. Let the rain of revival fall. Let the

> *rain of revival fall into our lives, O God. Make us more like You. Make us more like You, Jesus; more like You, Jesus. Lord, help us to go behind the veil. Help us to follow the Forerunner into the holy place, into the very presence of Almighty Jehovah, into the presence of our King, up onto the hill of the Lord.*

He is holding out the scepter, holding out the scepter in His hand. He says, "Take it from Me, My daughter; take it from Me, My son. Rule and reign; rule and reign on earth as it is in heaven. Rule and reign; rule and reign on earth as it is in heaven."

Heavenly rain is falling down, washing away all stains of darkness. Heavenly rain is falling down, disintegrating yokes of oppression, removing bondages and yokes of darkness. Oppression is going now. Generational curses of poverty are being dissolved in the name of the Lord. In the name of the Lord, the rain is falling—rain of revival, rain of refreshing, rain of the Kingdom, and the reign of the King. The rain of the King is within my heart.

> *Lord, we ask You to reign in our hearts. We ask You to reign in our lives. Take our hands, Father God. Lead us in the paths You've ordained for each of us. Let the rain fall. Let the gentle, healing rain fall. Let the beautiful rain fall. Let the desert bloom, O God. Let there be rivers in the desert. Let there be rivers in the desert. Let the rain of heaven come down. Restore this nation now. Let the rain fall upon the just and the evil alike, O God. You send down the rains from heaven, God. Let it rain upon the evil. Let the mercy of God rain down upon this nation,*

Prayers of Activation, Impartation, and Declarations of Glory

Lord. Forgive us, O God. Let Your rain of mercy fall, O Lord, on the just and the unjust. Let Your presence fall, O God. Turn the hearts of the kings; turn the hearts of the kings towards God Almighty. Let the rule and reign of God come, Lord. Refresh us, Lord. Send the fragrance of heaven. Lord, we bless what You are doing; we bless what You are doing; we bless what You are doing. Thank You for letting us come into the secret place for a few moments, God. Thank You, Papa. Thank You for Your love, God. Thank You for Your mercy. Thank You for Your grace, O Lord. We ask for mercy, Lord. We ask for mercy and not judgment, Lord. Let it rain, O God. Let it rain. Let a hard rain fall, O God; let a hard rain fall, let it fall, Lord. We worship You, O Lord. We worship You, Jehovah. We give You the glory, Lord. Thank You, Father.

Now, give the Lord a shout of praise!

Father, we thank You for Your word. Let it rain down, O God. Let it rain down from the heavenlies. Let the healing rains of heaven fall. Let them fall down upon me. Lord, we thank You that You are opening up Your good treasure of the heavens and raining down Your blessings. Father, thank You for raining down Your blessings. We lift up our hands to You, O God. We lift up our hands to You, O God. You are so good to us, Lord.

I believe the Lord is saying; "I am releasing an impartation to pass behind the veil." There is an impartation raining down, an impartation raining down. Step into the most holy place.

Step in without fear. Step in without trepidation, for the blood of Jesus Christ of Nazareth makes you righteous and holy. Holy is the Lord. He says, "Come to Me, My son. Come to Me, My daughter. Let Me wrap My arms of love around you. Let Me wrap My arms of love around you. Let Me kiss you with the kisses of My mouth. Gaze into My eyes of love. Let Me release you into your destiny."

There is impartation glory coming upon you as you are reading this now. Just reach up and receive the impartation for your destiny. Wherever you are, just by faith do a prophetic act: reach up and pull down the impartation for your destiny. "Even before you were knit together in your mother's womb," says the Lord, "I placed inside of you a strand of my DNA. It contains your destiny in Christ. It contains your destiny in the Kingdom. It contains your destiny in Me," says the Lord.

I see and decree that God changing your spiritual DNA right now. Ungodly spiritual DNA is being removed from many of you reading this book. It may feel funny but don't try to fight it; just press into it. Just receive it. God is changing your DNA. Many of you are actually having your minds renewed as the Spirit of God reaches into your mind and changes your DNA. "You will no longer think the way you have thought," says the Lord. "I'm creating a new mind in you." It's Psalm 51:10-12. He's creating new hearts within us. He's restoring new hearts.

> O God, thank You for that! Create new hearts within us, O God. Create a new heart within me, O Lord. Restore a steadfast spirit; restore a steadfast spirit—Your Spirit—within me, O God. Thank You, Lord.

Hearts are being renewed right now. Thus saith the Lord, "I restore the joy of your salvation; I restore the joy of your salvation." Many are being set free from religious bondage. Put off the cloak of religion and take on the mantle of Jesus. "Take My yoke," says the Lord. "Take My yoke," says the Lord, "for My burden is light." Many of you are going to feel as though a weight has been lifted off of your shoulders. It literally has. God is taking off heavy yokes and burdens. Heavy religious yokes are coming off right now in Jesus' name. God is placing freedom and grace upon you.

It is still raining, too. I see angels coming in with mantles. Angels are placing new mantles upon shoulders. You may feel that. Don't try to figure it out; just receive the impartation. Mantles of wisdom and revelation are being released.

God is anointing some of you for the healing ministry. I see the gifts of miracles being placed upon many of you reading this right now. I see an acceleration of ministries coming. "An acceleration, an acceleration, an acceleration," says the Lord. The Lord says, "Run to Me all of you who are weary and heavy laden, and I will give you rest."

I see God placing a mantle upon your shoulders to enter into His perfect rest. The rain is picking up again.

Thank You, God. The rains of heaven are washing us, cleansing us, restoring us. Let Your rains fall. Let Your rains fall. Someone is being healed in your shoulder right now; you might feel it pop. Healing of skeletal issues is happening right now—knees, shoulders, hips, fingers, backs, ankles, necks, spines being healed, in the name of

the Lord. Ears are being healed right now; it's going to feel like someone just turned to volume up on your ears. Father, thank You for healing ears.

I see and decree angels of healing and miracles being released. These are not regular angels of healing and miracles; these angels are being imparted and released to be with you wherever you go. You can expect these angels of miracles and healings to co-labor with you as you preach the Gospel. You may sense them behind you. You may feel the angels, God's angels, placing their hands upon your shoulders. And at times when these angels are released to co-labor with you, you will feel their hands rest upon your shoulders. And God will use them to speak a word in season to you, as you prophesy miracles and healings. Expect God to do great miracles, signs, and wonders by the power and anointing of the Holy Spirit of God Almighty.

You can enter into your secret place. Jesus said when you enter into your prayer closet, close the door behind you (Matthew 6:6). Expect to enter into that place when you pray; close the door and expect the very presence and glory from the heavenly realms to rain down upon you through the gates and windows of heaven. And then rest in that atmosphere of God's glory. Just rest in His glory and expect God to speak to you. Expect the Lord to give you revelation. Expect to discern the prayers of Jesus as He is seated at the right hand of the Father. Expect your life to be transformed.

*Father, we just give You the praise and the honor and the glory. We give **You**, Lord, the praise and the honor and*

*the glory. We give **You**, Lord, the praise and the honor and the glory. Father, we thank You for the ministry of the Holy Spirit. Holy Ghost, we bless You. Lord Jesus, thank You for visiting us. Papa God, Elohim, Jehovah, Father, we thank You for touching us. We give You all the glory. In Jesus' might name. Amen.*

Prayer of Salvation

Perhaps you would like to be born again and receive Jesus as your Lord and Savior now. Just pray this prayer out loud:

Father God, I believe that Jesus Christ is the Savior or Messiah. I believe that Jesus is the only begotten Son of God and that He died upon the Cross to make payment for my sins. I believe that Jesus was buried in an unused grave but that after three days He rose again to conquer death and sin. Lord, because I was born a human being, I was born a sinner. Lord, I ask You to forgive my sins now in the name of Jesus Christ of Nazareth. God, cover my sins with the atoning blood of Jesus and forgive me now. I receive Jesus Christ as my Savior and Lord. Amen.

Recommended Reading

For further study and understanding, we recommend these books:

The Sword of the Lord and the Rest of the Lord
    —KEVIN BASCONI

31 Word Decrees That Can Revolutionize Your Life
    —KEVIN BASCONI

Unlocking the Hidden Mysteries of the Powers of the Age to Come
    —*KEVIN BASCONI*

The Reality of Angelic Ministry Today trilogy:

Dancing With Angels 1:
How You Can Work With the Angels in Your Life
    —KEVIN BASCONI

Dancing With Angels 2:
The Role of the Holy Spirit and Open Heavens in Activating Your Angelic Visitations
    —KEVIN BASCONI

Dancing With Angels 3:
Angels in the Realms of Heaven
    —KEVIN BASCONI

The Apostle Paul: His Supernatural Walk With Jesus
—Kevin Basconi—Coming Soon

Come Up Higher
—Paul Cox, Aslan's Place

I Believe in Jesus
—Kenneth E. Hagin, Kenneth E. Hagin Ministries

Love the Way to Victory
—Kenneth E. Hagin, Kenneth E. Hagin Ministries

The Name of Jesus
—Kenneth E. Hagin, Kenneth E. Hagin Ministries

Good Morning Holy Spirit
—Benny Hinn, Thomas Nelson Publications

Secrets of the Argentine Revival
—Edward R. Miller, Peniel Publications

Open My Eyes Lord
—Gary Oates, Robert Lamb, Randy Clark, Open Heaven Publications

Churchquake
—C. Peter Wagner

School of the Seers
—Jonathan Welton, Destiny Image Publishers

Angels on Assignment
—Roland Buck, Whitaker House Publications

Angels: Knowing Their Purpose Releasing Power
—Charles Capps

About the Author

King of Glory Ministries International is all about the commission of Jesus Christ. The words of Isaiah 61 can be used to concisely summarize the call of the ministry.

> *The Spirit of the Lord GOD is upon Me, Because the Lord has anointed Me To preach good tidings to the poor; He has sent Me to heal the brokenhearted, To proclaim liberty to the captives, And the opening of the prison to those who are bound; To proclaim the acceptable year of the LORD, And the day of vengeance of our God; To comfort all who mourn, To console those who mourn in Zion, To give them beauty for ashes, The oil of joy for mourning, The garment of praise for the spirit of heaviness; That they may be called trees of righteousness, The planting of the Lord, that He may be glorified (Isaiah 61:1-3).*

Kevin and Kathy Basconi have sought to preach the Gospel of the Kingdom to the lost in many nations. As of this writing, we have visited thirty-three nations and five continents to proclaim the truth of Christ's total salvation and healing message or the Gospel of the Kingdom that Jesus instructed

His disciples to proclaim. (See Matthew 4:23; 9:35; 24:14.) We have preached to hundreds of thousands of people and seen tens of thousands make the decision to receive Jesus Christ as Lord and Savior. We continue to minister in Gospel outreaches as opportunity allows and as the Spirit leads. Kevin and Kathy also minister in churches, King of Glory Ministries International Schools, and conference meetings in various nations. They have also begun to develop the King of Glory Ministries International (iMEC); International Ministry Equipping Center in Moravian Falls, North Carolina. For more information about the (iMEC) visit our web page.

The other critical calling of King of Glory Ministries International is to minister the love of the Father to widows and orphans. This humanitarian aspect of our call can be defined in the scriptures of James 1:27 and Psalm 68:5. James 1:27 tells us this: "Pure and undefiled religion before God and the Father is this: to visit orphans and widows in their trouble, and to keep oneself unspotted from the world." God has birthed in Kevin and Kathy a heart to minister in deed and not word alone. We also see this aspect of the Father's heart in Psalm 68:5: "A father of the fatherless, a defender of widows, Is God in His holy habitation." (See the Orphanage Tab on ministry's web page for more information about this important aspect of King of Glory Ministries International.)

The ministry is punctuated by many miracles, healings, and signs and wonders that confirm the word of God. They live in the mountains of North Carolina where they pursue a lifestyle of intimacy with Jesus. Kevin is an internationally published author and artist. He the author of several books, including

About the Author

The Sword of the Lord and the Rest of the Lord and the trilogy, *The Reality of Angelic Ministry Today.* Kevin has been graced by God to see into the spiritual realm for over a decade. Kevin is also called to equip the church to operate in the seer anointing and to understand how to enter into the presence and glory of God. Kevin is an ordained minister accredited with World Ministry Fellowship of Plano, Texas. King of Glory Ministries International is connected to the apostolic leadership of Pastor Alan and Carol Koch of Christ Triumphant Church located In Lee's Summit, Missouri.

Contact the Author

Kevin and Kathy would love to hear your testimonies about how this book has impacted your walk with Christ. To submit testimonies contact them by e-mail.
info@kingofgloryministries.org

King of Glory Ministries International
is available to teach the material covered in this book
in much greater depth in our
School of the Seers—Level One and Level Two

These schools are also available in DVD and CD formats.

For more information or to order additional books
And other resources visit our web page at:

www.kingofgloryministries.org
Email: info@kingofgloryministries.org.
Phone: 336-818-1210 or 828-320-3502

Mailing Address:
King of Glory Ministries International
PO Box 903, Moravian Falls, NC 28654

Prophetic Worship CD

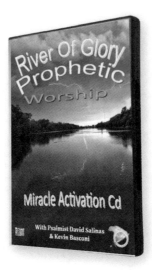

This worship Cd, *River Of Glory Prophetic Worship*, was recorded live on Saturday, November 2nd, 2014 at Christ Triumphant Church. (All sales benefit widows and orphans). We believe that the glory that was present in this session is attached to this digitally re-mastered recording. Psalmist David Salinas ushered in the glory of God during the worship in this meeting. Then Kevin was actually taken up into the throne room. Kevin began to decree the things that he was seeing in the heavenly realms. We believe that as Kevin decrees the supernatural things that he witnessed in the Throne room on this Mp3, you can also receive your miracle and healing as you listen and soak to the worship and spontaneous decrees of heaven.

$19.99

SALE $12.00

Activating Your 20/20 Spiritual Vision CD

In this message, *Activating Your 20/20 Spiritual Vision*, Kevin shares several keys that can help you to establish your seer gift and your 20/20 spiritual senses. It is imperative the we become diligent to hear the voice of the Lord and to see what God is doing in our lives at this hour. It is imperative the you develop and build up your ability to discern both good and evil each and every day according to the principle of Hebrews 5:14; Solid food belongs to those who are mature, those who by reason of use have their senses exercised to discern both good and evil. God is seeking to heal and open the spiritual eyes and spiritual ears of His people at this hour. We believe that this message and the prayer of impartation at the end can help spark such a supernatural metamorphosis in your life too! You can learn to discern and activate your 20/20 spiritual senses and vision enabling you to recreate Christ in your sphere of influence. Amen!

$12.00

SALE $10.00

Apostolic Love
CD

This digitally mastered Cd teaching outlines your right and ability to become a royal priest after the order of Melchizedek. The Blood is Jesus Christ and the Apostolic Love of God opens this door to the heavenly realms to each of us.

$12.00

SALE $10.00

Moravian Falls School Of The Seers Box Set 8 CD

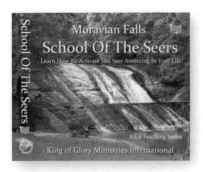

This 8 cd box set is designed to empower you to activate the seer anointing in your life. God created each of us in His image, and as such our spiritual DNA is designed to see and to be seers. We are created to have intimacy and communion with God. We are created to see and hear the Lord clearly. These teaching will help you to activate your ability to hear and see from the realms of heaven clearly. When you activate your seer gifting it can be life changing! This set includes these teachings by Kevin & Kathy Basconi:

Lesson #1 - Disc #1 - What Is The Seer Anointing Lesson #1 - Disc #2 - What Is The Seer Anointing Part #2 Lesson #2 - Disc #3 - Understanding The Seer Anointing Lesson #2 - Disc #4 - Understanding The Seer Anointing Part #2 Lesson #3 - Disc #5 The Seer Anointing & The Gift of Discerning Of Spirits Lesson #4 - Disc #6 The Seer Anointing & Open Heavens Lesson #5 - Disc #7 Activating the Seer Anointing - Part #2 Lesson #5 - Disc #8 Prayers of Impartation To Receive The Seer Anointing - Part #2

$85.00
SALE $65.00

Cultivating The Glory
3 DVD School

This 3 DVD School set is designed to help you understand and activate the glory of God to work in your life. Understanding how to live in the glory realms can transform your life! In these teaching DVDs Kevin shares amazing testimonies of supernatural encounters with God's tangible Shekinah glory!

~~$29.99~~

SALE $24.00

Sowing into the Glory DVD

In this DVD teaching Kevin shares another powerful testimony about how you can activate supernatural prosperity in your life and circumstances when you learn to Sow Into The Glory! This message was birthed when Kevin experienced an extended season and visitation of God's glory. The Lord also allowed Kevin to understand how God releases powerful angels from the heavenly realms to help empower those who are seeking to further His kingdom. This dynamic is one aspect of the mantle or anointing of Melchizedek that the Lord is releasing to His friends at this hour. Kevin and Kathy experienced an extraordinary angelic visitation on Sunday, April 29th, 2012. When this angel of the Lord manifested so did a tangible purple glory cloud. In that atmosphere of God's glory, creative miracles began to occur, and over the course of the next year Kevin was given revelation about these Kingdom principles in relationship to supernatural provision and creative miracles.

~~$15.00~~

SALE $12.00

The Powers Of The Age To Come & The Glory Of God CD

This message, *The Powers Of The Age To Come & The Glory Of God* was birthed in revival. Learn to live in the power of God, in God's Love, and with Gods healing and redeeming power in your life and in your sphere of influence! Learning about the powers of the age to come is crucial for every believer today. Our prayer is that this message will help you to step into the greater works of John 14:10-12, and activate the power of the age to come in your life.

~~$12.00~~

SALE $9.00

Discerning & Overcoming The Accuser of the Brethren CD

This 2 Cd message, *Discerning & Overcoming The Accuser of the Brethren*, can transform your life through the anointed Word of God! The anointing breaks the heavy yokes and burdens of darkness and deception. You can learn to set yourself free from yokes of darkness and oppression and as you do your life will be transformed! You can go from hopelessness to hope, from sickness to health, from poverty to prosperity.

~~$12.00~~

SALE $9.00

The Sword of the Lord
& The Rest of the Lord

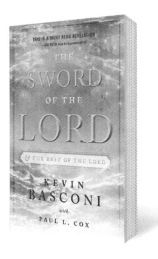

This book *The Sword of the Lord & The Rest of the Lord* was birthed on the Day of Atonement in 2011 and completed on the Day of Atonement in 2012.

Kevin was taken up into the heavenly realms and began to see a tremendous storm full of ominous black clouds moving across the horizon. After some time Kevin witnessed the sky split open and saw the Lord Jesus Christ decent towards the earth upon a mighty white stallion. Jesus was accompanied by millions upon millions of angelic beings who were arrayed for battle. The Lord of Hosts and these millions of angels began to confront the darkness and the billowing storm below. This book is a vivid depiction of those events.

Co-Authored with Paul Cox.

~~$20.00~~

SALE $15.00

Unlocking the Hidden Mysteries of the Seer Anointing

This book contains the teachings the revelations that the Lord has given Kevin over the last 12 year about the seer anointing. We are living in a God ordained moment of time when the seer realm is being released by grace to God's friends (whosoever). This book is designed to help God's people unlock the hidden mysteries of the seer anointing in their lives by understanding the idiosyncrasies of the seer anointing in a Christ centered and sound biblical manner. It is a very through biblical teaching that also is replete with dozens of prayers of activation for the reader (seers).

~~$20.00~~

SALE $15.00

Understanding The Shabbat and Rosh Chodesh CD

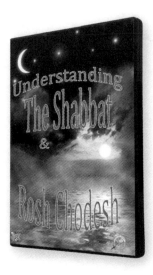

In this double Cd teaching; *A Practical Understanding of The Shabbat and Rosh Chodesh*, Kevin Shares his heart and a basic look at the weekly Sabbath rest and the monthly appointed time of Rosh Chodesh. This scriptural teaching can give you a basic overview of these two important appointed times to come and present yourself before the Lord. There are weekly and monthly times that the Scriptures call us to come before the Lord to receive His blessings and to honor or hallow the Lord. This understanding is a basic key to entering into the rest of the Lord and receiving the supernatural favor of God.

~~$12.00~~
SALE $9.00

The Seer Anointing &
The Blessings of Psalm 24 CD

In this 2 Cd activation message, *The Seer Anointing & The Blessings of Psalm 24*, Kevin Basconi shares several powerful supernatural encounters concerning the seer anointing. These testimonies have taken place over the last decade as the Lord has released to Kevin understanding and revelation about the seer anointing. On February 25th, 2014 Kevin experienced a powerful angelic visitation in Moravian Falls, North Carolina. In the glory realms that resulted from this supernatural experience Kevin received revelatory understanding from the Spirit of the Lord from Psalm 24. In this message Kevin shares that prophetic word about God's imminent intentions to empower His friends (seers)..

~~$12.00~~

SALE $9.00

Unlocking the Hidden Mysteries of the Seer Anointing

Look inside ↓

This book contains the teachings the revelations that the Lord has given Kevin over the last 12 year about the seer anointing. We are living in a God ordained moment of time when the seer realm is being released by grace to God's friends (whosoever). This book is designed to help God's people unlock the hidden mysteries of the seer anointing in their lives by understanding the idiosyncrasies of the seer anointing in a Christ centered and sound biblical manner. It is a very through biblical teaching that also is replete with dozens of prayers of activation for the reader (seers).

http://www.amazon.com/dp/B00I2D6WX6

Kindle price $9.99

The Sword of the Lord
& The Rest of the Lord

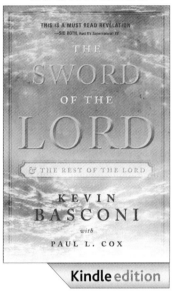

This book *The Sword of the Lord & The Rest of the Lord* was birthed on the Day of Atonement in 2011 and completed on the Day of Atonement in 2012. Kevin was taken up into the heavenly realms and began to see a tremendous storm full of ominous black clouds moving across the horizon. After some time Kevin witnessed the sky split open and saw the Lord Jesus Christ decent towards the earth upon a mighty white stallion. Jesus was accompanied by millions upon millions of angelic beings who were arrayed for battle. The Lord of Hosts and these millions of angels began to confront the darkness and the billowing storm below. This book is a vivid depiction of those events. Co-Authored with Paul Cox.

http://www.amazon.com/dp/B00CR2RWR8

Kindle price $9.99

31 Word Decrees
That Will Revolutionize Your Life

This new 2014 version has been edited and revised! It includes a new bonus word Decree! Forward by Paul Cox.

This little book was birthed or "breathed into existence" by the Holy Spirit. Kevin Basconi has been speaking God's word over his life since he was saved, and delivered from a lifestyle of addiction and sin. In short order the Lord transformed Kevin's life and took him from poverty to prosperity, and from bondage to freedom, from sickness to health.

http://www.amazon.com/dp/B00HY3MJ1Y

Kindle price $7.99